Fortress • 66

The Castles of Henry VIII

Peter Harrington · Illustrated by Brian Delf

Series editors Marcus Cowper and Nikolai Bogdanovic

D1158924

First published in 2007 by Osprey Publishing
Midland House, West Way, Botley, Oxford OX2 0PH, UK
443 Park Avenue South, New York, NY 10016, USA
E-mail: info@ospreypublishing.com

ISBN 978 184603 130 4

Editorial by Ilios Publishing, Oxford, UK (www.iliospublishing.com)
Cartography: Map Studio, Romsey, UK
Typeset in Monotype Gill Sans and ITC Stone Serif
Design by Ken Vail Graphic Design, Cambridge, UK
Index by Alan Thatcher
Originated by United Graphic Pte Ltd, Singapore
Printed in China through Bookbuilders

07 08 09 10 11   10 9 8 7 6 5 4 3 2 1

A CIP catalogue record for this book is available from the British Library.

FOR A CATALOGUE OF ALL BOOKS PUBLISHED BY OSPREY MILITARY AND AVIATION
PLEASE CONTACT:

Osprey Direct, c/o Random House Distribution Center, 400 Hahn Road,
Westminster, MD 21157
Email: info@ospreydirect.com

Osprey Direct UK, P.O. Box 140, Wellingborough, Northants, NN8 2FA, UK
E-mail: info@ospreydirect.co.uk

www.ospreypublishing.com

Acknowledgements and image credits

The author would like to acknowledge the assistance of several
regional friends and correspondents for providing images and
drawings of some of the castles, particularly Geoffrey Boot (Kent),
Peter Laurie (Dorset), Peter Wraight (Kent and Sussex), Stephen
Wood (Hampshire and the Isle of Wight) and Andrew Saunders.
The following abbreviations are used in the image captions in this
book, to indicate the source of each:

ASKB   Anne S. K. Brown Military Collection, Brown University
       Library
GB   Geoffrey Boot
PH   Peter Harrington
PL   Peter Laurie
PW   Peter Wraight
SAL   Society of Antiquaries of London
SW   Stephen Wood

A note on nomenclature

The artillery fortifications built during the reign of Henry VIII
are referred to in the present text as castles or forts. In the
contemporary record, the terms castles, fortresses, bulwarks and
blockhouses are used interchangeably. For instance, the castle at
Portland is sometimes referred to as 'Portland Bulwark', while
some of the corresponding earthworks built adjacent to the
Downs castles and at Dover are also referred to as bulwarks. In
their modern classification as ancient monuments, the structures
are listed as castles. Some writers feel that the term 'fort' best
describes these structures and at least one author has used
the term 'fort' in naming the various places, e.g. Fort Walmer,
Fort Deal, Fort Hurst, and so on.

Artist's note

Readers may care to note that the original paintings from which
the colour plates in this book were prepared are available for
private sale. All reproduction copyright whatsoever is retained
by the Publishers. All enquiries should be addressed to:

Brian Delf
7 Burcot Park
Burcot
Abingdon
Oxon
OX14 3DH
UK

The Publishers regret that they can enter into no correspondence
upon this matter.

The Fortress Study Group (FSG)

The object of the FSG is to advance the education of the public
in the study of all aspects of fortifications and their armaments,
especially works constructed to mount or resist artillery. The FSG
holds an annual conference in September over a long weekend
with visits and evening lectures, an annual tour abroad lasting
about eight days, and an annual Members' Day.
The FSG journal *FORT* is published annually, and its newsletter
Casemate is published three times a year. Membership is
international. For further details, please contact:

The Secretary, c/o 6 Lanark Place, London W9 1BS, UK
Website: www.fsgfort.com

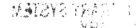

Contents

Introduction

A unique group of masonry artillery forts survives along the southern coast of England. These forts represent the last form of castle building in the country, and they owe their very existence to the political events surrounding a reigning monarch, Henry VIII, his desire for a successor which impacted on his marital situation, and the subsequent hostilities that resulted from his actions and domestic policies. These fortified buildings are quite different from their medieval predecessors in design and layout, and their influences can be traced directly to developments on the continent in the previous century.

Henry VIII inherited from his father, Henry VII, a great ambition to make England a strong power in Europe when he became king in 1509. To achieve this, he embarked on several military campaigns that equalized the balance of power

Marital problems and an obsession with the succession created a situation that Henry VIII (1491–1547) had not anticipated. His break with the Papacy over his divorce from Catherine of Aragon led to the destruction of Church infrastructure in England, and a scheme to fortify the southern coasts to meet the consequences. (ASKB)

with his French counterpart, Francis I. The year 1519 saw the ascendancy of Charles V of Spain as Emperor of the Holy Roman Empire. Three years later, Henry joined Charles in a further attack upon France, but with Charles's victory over the French at Pavia in 1525, Henry became concerned that the emperor himself would control most of Europe. So concerned was he that he switched allegiance and made peace with France. The Pope similarly backed France against the emperor who immediately invaded Italy in 1527, sacking Rome. With financial backing from Henry, Francis set out for Italy but his campaign ended in disaster leaving Henry and England almost bankrupt.

In 1509, the emperor's aunt, Catherine of Aragon, had married the young Henry in what was a prearranged marriage in order to firmly cement the alliance between Henry VII and Ferdinand and Isabella of Spain. Catherine had been married to Henry's oldest brother, Arthur: the 15-year-old prince succumbed to the plague in April of the following year leaving Henry as sole heir to the throne, and Catherine already a widow at 17. In order for Henry to marry his former sister-in-law, he had to secure a papal dispensation, which he was

Thomas Cromwell (1485?–1540), Henry's principal architect of the dissolution of the monasteries, was the chief organizer of the fortification scheme, but later fell out of grace with the king. He was executed without trial by order of the king shortly after being created Earl of Essex. (ASKB)

able to do. By all accounts the first years of marriage went well, at least until the issue of an heir became paramount. Although the queen conceived at least six times in the first nine years of marriage, she failed to produce the desired son. She had two miscarriages and once delivered a stillborn girl. Two sons died, the first only a few hours after birth, the second within a few weeks. Catherine's only gift to her monarch was a daughter, Mary, born in 1516, who would go on to become Queen Mary I, a staunch Catholic and better known as 'Bloody Mary' for her harsh treatment of Protestant heretics.

Frustrated and disappointed at the lack of a male heir, Henry nonetheless remained devoted to Catherine for 18 years, although he carried on several affairs with other women, one of whom was Mary Boleyn, elder sister of Anne. The situation came to a head in 1527 with the 'King's Great Matter' – the succession. Catherine was now past her prime at 42, while the 36-year-old Henry was still in full vigour. In that year, the king had become enamoured with Anne Boleyn. Anne apparently resisted Henry's advances until assured of becoming his wife. Frustrated, he began to reflect on the state of his marriage with Catherine and the failed attempt at producing a male heir and decided upon one solution – a divorce. Only the Pope could grant this, but he was under the control of Emperor Charles, Henry's current enemy and Catherine's nephew. Divorce proceedings were started but dragged on for six years, and the impasse was only broken when Henry declared that he was breaking with the Church of Rome to become the head of a new Protestant church, a Church of England. This sparked a period of anti-clericalism in England and provided Henry with the opportunity of refilling the royal coffers. Around the countryside were numerous monastic houses, symbols of Rome, and by dissolving these religious foundations, he could redistribute their lands and wealth. Henry finally divorced Catherine in 1533, probably a few months after marrying Anne.

The king appointed a layman, Thomas Cromwell, as his vicar-general in 1534 with special authority to visit the monastic houses, and to bring them into line with the new order of things. Henry had already decided upon the fate of the monasteries and they were doomed prior to any visitations, which began in a systematic fashion during the summer of 1535. By the end of 1536 it was estimated that 376 religious houses had been closed; and by 1540 when

The embarkation of Henry VIII at Dover on May 31, 1520, to meet Francis I. Two circular towers can be seen in the foreground. These represent some of the early 16th-century defences of Dover harbour. (ASKB)

the last of the abbeys had been dissolved, approximately 8,000 persons had been turned out of the monasteries, abbeys, friaries and convents. The annual value of the entire properties was estimated at over £200,000 but this figure excludes the value of the possessions removed from the religious houses.

Henry's actions only hardened the resolve of the Pope and Charles against him. France, too, was keen on getting back at Henry but he was able to keep the two sides apart until 1538 when the emperor and Francis signed a ten-year truce. An invasion aimed at re-establishing the Pope's authority in England now seemed not only inevitable but imminent, an event for which the country was woefully unprepared.

In the wake of the (quickly suppressed) northern uprising against the dissolution, known as the Pilgrimage of Grace, maps were produced by Henry's military engineers of ports on the south and east coast of England. They were acting for commissioners who had been appointed to 'search and defend' the coastline. Using the maps and surveys, it was now Henry's intention to construct a systematic chain of forts and batteries along the south and east coasts particularly covering the major ports and estuaries, in order to prevent a hostile invasion from the Continent. This project was known as 'the King's Device'. Fortunately for Henry, the threat that seemed so real in 1538 passed as quickly as it came, and by the time the first castles had been completed, England had little to fear from any such military enterprises. Nevertheless, the fortification scheme continued, and a second series of structures was erected in the early 1540s as a contingency against any future attacks.

It is important to remember that the Henrician castles that exist today along the south coast of England are the surviving vestiges of a much broader scheme involving not only masonry structures but also chains of earthwork embankments, ditches and bulwarks, constructed to protect the coastline of Britain from Berwick on the Anglo-Scottish border down to Kent, along the south coast, and up to south Wales. Even the English possessions in northern France around Calais were included. Therefore the castles should not be seen in isolation but in the context of a complex fortification system.

Chronology

1509 Henry succeeds his father, Henry VII, as Henry VIII.
Marriage of Catherine of Aragon to Henry.

1533 Henry VIII divorces Catherine of Aragon.

1534 Thomas Cromwell appointed vicar-general with authority
to visit monastic houses to bring them in line with the
new order.

1536 Suppression of a revolt in northern England known as the
Pilgrimage of Grace.

1538 Holy Roman Emperor Charles V and Francis I of France sign
a ten-year truce.

1539 Invasion scare; first Henrician castles begun.

1540 Final monasteries and abbeys dissolved.

1544 English capture Boulogne (September).

1545 French attack in the Solent and land on the Isle of
Wight (July).

1547 Death of Henry VIII.

The location of the various castles
and blockhouses constructed during
the fortification phases between
1539 and 1547.

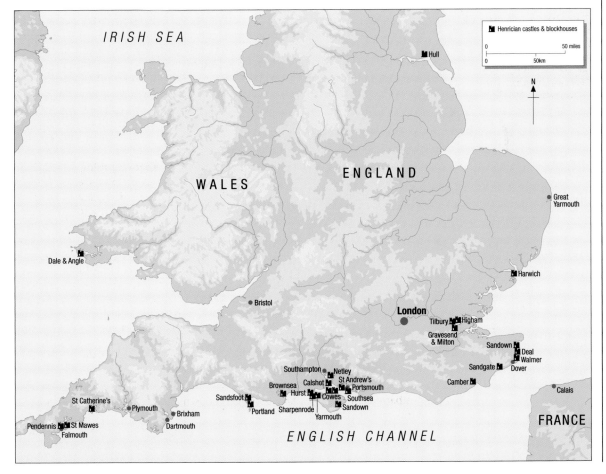

A site chronology

Key: BH = blockhouse; C = castle/fort

Site	Commenced	Completed	Cost (rounded)
1539 device programme			
East & West Cowes (BH)	March/April 1539	March 1542 (?)	Unknown
Sandgate (C)	March 1539	October 1540	£5,584
Sandown, Kent (C)	April 1539	Autumn 1540	£27,092 (includes costs for Walmer and Deal)
Walmer (C)	April 1539	Autumn 1540	See Sandown
Deal (C)	April 1539	Autumn 1540	See Sandown
Calshot (C)	Spring 1539	Autumn 1540	Unknown
Camber I (C)	1539	Autumn 1540	£5,660
Gravesend (BH)	August 1539	March 1540	£1,072
Milton (BH)	1539	1545 (?)	£1,072
Higham (BH)	1539	1540	£980
East & West Tilbury (BH)	1539	1546 (?)	£506
Portland (C)	Summer 1539	1541	£4,964
Sandsfoot (C)	Summer 1539	1541(?)	£3,887
St Mawes (C)	April 1540	September 1545 (?)	£5,018
Pendennis (C)	October 1540	1545 (?)	£5,614
Hurst (C)	February 1541	January 1544	£3,200+
Camber II (C)	1542	1543	£10,000
1544 device programme			
Southsea (C)	1544	1544	c. £3,100
Netley (C)	1544 (?)	1544 (?)	Unknown
Brownsea (C)	1545	1547	Unknown
Sandown, Isle of Wight (C)	April 1545	September 1545	£2,400
Yarmouth (C)	May 1547	November 1547	£6,542

Design and development

Fortification theory and practice

To search for the origins and influences that inspired Henry VIII's castles and fortifications built between 1539 and 1547, there are two lines of evidence to follow: the state of fortification in Britain in the late 15th and early 16th century; and the situation on the Continent in the first three decades of the 16th century relating to emerging ideas of fortification.

Artillery had been in use in Britain since the 14th century. Edward III had employed primitive guns during his Scottish campaign of 1327, and three years later the besieged garrison of Berwick was exposed to firearms, albeit on a very limited level. Within a decade or so, larger guns made of cast iron began to be used, but these bombards were still ineffective as siege weapons. The impact of gunpowder artillery on fortified structures in terms of modifications was negligible for over a century. In fact, the only concession to the new form was the addition of holes knocked through walls for guns to fire through. These enlarged arrow-slits, known as gun-ports or loops, usually covered entrances, and early examples can be seen at various castles including Berry Pomeroy in Devon, and Cooling Castle, Kent, and on the West Gate of Canterbury, Kent. The castle at Ravenscraig, Fife, Scotland, built around the middle of the 15th century, reflects some of the new continental ideas of fortification, principally French. Here, widely splayed gun-ports were constructed within the massive semi-circular towers that flanked the entrance.

Although Continental ideas of artillery fortification were slow to catch on in Britain, by the late 15th century some fortifications were being constructed with artillery in mind. One example is Dartmouth Castle guarding the entrance to the River Dart on the south coast of Devon. When completed in 1495, it was regarded as the most advanced fortified structure in the country. Here the gun-ports were not afterthoughts but deliberately planned features facing the estuary, while the main tower was designed for the offensive use of guns rather than merely to defend the castle. Seven rectangular openings, four near the waterline and three above, were equipped with shutters and splayed internally to allow the gunners to move their weapons from side to side. In addition there are 11 small, splayed, square openings on the ground floor to accommodate hand-guns.

Besides Dartmouth Castle and its sister castle at Kingswear constructed across the River Dart in 1491, few artillery fortifications were built on the English coast in the following decades. The country was at peace for most of the time, with the exception of the volatile Anglo-Scottish border, so there was little need for coastal defence. Bayard's Cove tower was constructed nearby to guard the town of Dartmouth probably between 1509 and 1510. Semi-circular in plan, it had thick walls pierced by a single line of 11 gun-ports with internal splays, above which was a wall-walk and parapet. Two years later saw Henry's

Three early gun-ports at Berry Pomeroy Castle, Devon. These superimposed openings consist of two round holes for hand-guns above a double-splayed rectangular opening for a small cannon mounted on a stock. (PH)

invasion of France, and with it a plan for the defence of the south-west coast. The resulting fortifications were temporary in nature, consisting of nothing more than earthworks and ditches built by local people. In 1522–23, renewed conflict with France saw the construction of some new defences along the south coast, including a blockhouse at Brixham, and Worsley's Tower across the Solent from the site of the future Henrician castle at Hurst Point. This was a squat octagonal tower, 19 feet high and 26 feet round, with the main armament probably situated on the roof, firing through embrasures. There may have been further gun-ports near ground level. In Cornwall, St Catherine's Castle was built in 1536 to protect Fowey harbour from French invasion. It was a precursor to the device forts, consisting of a circular tower with two storeys of gun-ports at ground level.

In searching for European antecedents of the Henrician style of fortification, the name of Albrecht Dürer has been raised. He had served as an advisor on the fortifications of Antwerp in 1520–21, and later was the author of one of the first two books dealing with fortifications, the other being by Machiavelli. In *Etliche underricht zu befestigung der Stett, Schlosz, und flecken* published in Nürenberg in 1527, Dürer included discussion and engraved plates promoting the curved bastion and an ideal coastal fortification entirely circular in form. Some writers have identified elements in the Henrician forts reflecting Dürer's ideas, while others have dismissed his influence, suggesting it was doubtful that his works could have been read in England. The latter argument cannot be proved and certainly someone like Stefan von Haschenperg, one of the king's engineers, coming as he did from Germany, would most likely have been aware of Dürer's study. However, the fact that some of the ideas proposed by Dürer – such as smoke vents, curved parapets and widely splayed external embrasures – had already been employed in England and France, suggests that he was not the primary influence behind Henry's castles.

In Italy, rounded bastions were still being constructed as late as the mid 1530s at Assisi, while at Cortona round corner towers were built in 1543. The ideas of the Roman military engineer Vitruvius, who claimed that blows against round towers would not harm them while angled masonry would be shattered, still served as a guiding principle, although questions were beginning to be raised concerning issues of flanking fire and dead ground.

Constructed between 1481 and 1495, Dartmouth Castle was the most advanced fortification designed for artillery. Situated on the west bank of the River Dart in Devon, its cannons fired from ports near the water level, and although fixed could cover the whole estuary. (PH)

While English knowledge of Continental practices might have been limited at the outset of the building programme due to lack of first-hand experience, the transition of fortifications from the round towers and bastions at the beginning of the scheme in 1539 to the angular bastions by the mid 1540s clearly demonstrated an increasing awareness acquired from direct observation of fortifications on the Continent. This may have occurred during the king's military expeditions to France during this decade.

A device for the fortification of the realm

Henry's national defence scheme for fortifying the harbours and coasts of southern England has been called 'the Device'. In fact, it was just one of many plans or 'devices' on the agenda for the Parliament of 1539; others included a device 'for the poor people in this realm', a device 'for the unity of religion', and a device 'that one man shall not have too many offices in Wales, nor the leading of too many men'.

The programme has been described by the late Brian St John O'Neil as 'the one scheme of comprehensive coastal defence ever attempted in England before modern times'. Initially, the plan called for the fortification of certain points along the coastline from the Thames to the Solent, as well as the English-controlled French towns of Calais and Guisnes. This went as follows:

Detail of one of the towers guarding Dover harbour, showing splayed gun-ports and rounded parapets. These features anticipated some of the characteristics of the Henrician structures. (ASKB)

> Device by the King for three new bulwarks to be made in the Downs and other places on the frontiers of the sea, viz.: – In the Downs, 3 blockhouses or bulwarks … In the Camber, 1 blockhouse … At Calshottes Point, 1 blockhouse … The bulwarks in the Thames…

A 'Rembrance' written in Thomas Cromwell's hand sometime later notes that letters should be sent to the captain of the Isle of Wight 'for the fortification of the castle and isle there', but there is no mention in 1539 of additional defences for the harbours of Portland or Falmouth which would not be planned and constructed until the following year.

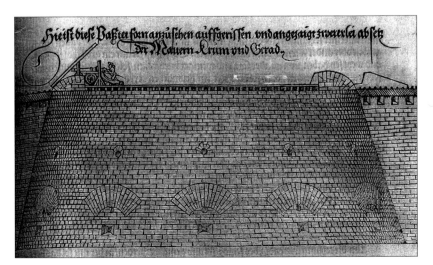

Albrecht Dürer's treatise on fortifications entitled *Etliche underricht zu befestigung der Stett, Schlosz, und flecken* was published in 1527. Dürer's study may have been the first printed book devoted to artillery fortification. He proposed such developments as round bastions with casemates, curved parapets and smoke vents, as shown here. (ASKB)

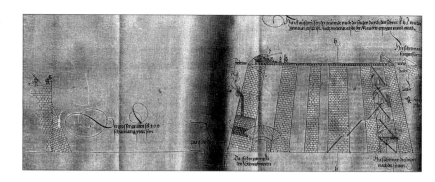

Another plate from Dürer's treatise, showing a design for a tall, tapering circular tower with staircases, smoke vents, rounded parapets and ditch. The study was a synthesis of pervading ideas then current on the Continent. (ASKB)

In addition, the plan called for the appointment of commissioners to travel around the coastline bordering the English Channel and report on existing defences as well as to locate areas suitable for the building of new fortifications. For instance, the Lord Admiral, the Earl of Southampton, went to Portsmouth in April 1539 and then reconnoitered the area around Southampton Water and the Solent. Other districts were examined, including Dorset and the West Country, which was inspected by Sir John Russell.

Engineers

The design of Henry's artillery forts has been attributed to various engineers. Some of this is based on documentary evidence, some of it on supposition. It is clear that a number of individuals were involved in the architecture of the buildings but they are not all easily identified. There is a note from Cromwell requesting that letters should be written to 'expert men in every shire near the sea to view the coasts and advise about fortification of places where there is danger of invasion', no doubt a reference to the appointment of commissioners referred to above. Some of these commissioners might have been trained in the art of fortification, as perhaps were some of the many persons identified in the records as being involved in the construction of the various structures. For example, money was paid to a certain Robert Lorde for the 'new building of the castles, bulwarks and fortress upon the Downes and at Dover', and similarly to John Mille 'to make fortresses at East Cowe, West Cowe, and Calshot, Hants'. Anthony Awger was paid for works at Dover in 1541. Richard Cavendish is credited with devising the king's bulwark at Dover in 1538, and in 1543 was described as 'a discreet person in fortification'.

In a letter to Cromwell written on March 20, 1539, William Earl of Southampton and William Lord St John mention that they had 'taken a view of our platt [plan] for the tower at Calshotispoynt', and later state that they had 'devised' towers at East and West Cowes and Calshot. They made recommendations to transform old Worsley's Tower opposite Hurst Point, 'so that there also we [have devised] a fourth tower to be made, wich [shall be] wonderfully well defended by the [country] adjoyning, wich is part of Hampshire and very populose'. In fact, the king himself once referred to the Earl of Southampton as an 'expert' in fortification. In the initial scheme laid out early in 1539, several names of possible architects are listed, including Sir Christopher Morris. Another member of the court, Thomas Howard, Duke of Norfolk, states in a letter of June 27, 1545 that he had 'devised bulwarks and platforms for ordnance and ramparts' at Great Yarmouth on the coast of Norfolk.

Whether such men were merely builders following the directions from others or had some input on the design is not clear. One continental engineer by the name of Stefan von Haschenperg is identified in the documents as being directly involved with the work at two sites, Camber and Sandgate. The king himself took a keen interest and may have made suggestions on design. Towards the end of Henry's reign, John Rogers and Richard Lee are known to have contributed designs of some of the later forts and those on the Continent.

Stefan von Haschenperg

It has been suggested that the lack of trained English engineers meant that the king had to look abroad for expertise. One such person was Stefan von Haschenperg, or Stephen the Almain as he is sometimes referred to. His name is closely linked with some of the design elements at Sandgate and Camber castles as well as the earthwork fortifications linking the forts in the Downs, although his true skills lay in land surveying. Apparently hailing from the Moravian region of Germany, it is not known when 'Master Stevyn the devysour' came to England, or under whose sponsorship, but his name first appears in a letter written in Latin to Thomas Cromwell from Deal, Kent, dated April 12, 1539 and over the next year he was directly involved with the various sites. His presence at Deal was related to the construction of the earthwork defences, where he is identified as 'surveyor of the four bulwarks upon the Downs otherwise called Devysor of the Woorkes ther'.

An aerial view of Sandgate Castle, Kent, showing the central keep, now a private residence but originally a Martello tower. The gatehouse and the low walls of two of the external bastions can be seen, while the third has been partially destroyed by coastal erosion. (GB)

Haschenperg visited Camber on several occasions during the latter half of 1539 to supervise the remodelling of the keep and was at Folkestone and Sandgate at other times. At Camber he attempted to create a fortification inspired by some of the developments coming out of Italy: it was low in profile with flankers and had a surrounding earthwork glacis serving as an outer defence, although the angled bastion was noticeable by its absence. Yet within 18 months his work had been superseded by more traditional forms with a heightened keep and four stirrup-shaped towers.

The extant building accounts for Sandgate cover the period March–December 1539 and January–October 1540, and Haschenperg's name appears frequently on the ledgers. However, his prior commitments at Camber, the Downs and occasionally in London, meant that he was rarely on site. The last account signed by him at Sandgate is dated March 21, 1540. The next year found him at Carlisle working on the new fortifications, and two years later he was apparently dismissed possibly, due to the view that he was incompetent as a military engineer. Another explanation appeared in a document of July 17, 1543: 'Stephen Almain [sic] having long had charge of certain buildings and fortifications, appeared to have behaved lewdly and spent great treasure to no purpose'. On several occasions, he clashed with colleagues over various construction issues and was apparently better suited as a land surveyor than as a designer of fortifications. As evidence of this were his plans for roofing the round towers at Sandgate with canvas, pitch and tar, which smacks of ignorance. His assistant, Thomas Cockys, wrote to Cromwell from Sandgate on this matter on September 3, 1539:

> The castle at Sandgate, within your lordship of Folkestone, is well brought forward. The three towers are ready to be covered; which Stephen the Almain, deviser of the said Castle, would have covered with canvas, pitch, and tar. Thinks lead would be better, of which there is enough to cover the whole castle.

By the time of his dismissal, most of the fortifications had been completed and the king clearly had no further need of his services.

The king's interest

Henry VIII shared a great interest in the latest developments in the military science of the day and was fascinated with artillery and fortifications. Beyond the various military treatises that made their way to the court, Henry's only opportunity of studying some of the new developments first-hand was during

Two earthen bulwarks with ditch and bank connecting Deal Castle with Sandown Castle, Kent, 1539

his French campaign of 1544, when he would have seen some of the new fortress designs. In particular, Italian ideas of the angular bastion were beginning to make their appearance. The later Henrician forts such as at Southsea and Yarmouth clearly reflect some of these new principles and could well be the result of experience gained during the campaign.

As for Henry's direct involvement in the planning and design of the fortifications, the evidence is tantalizing. In 1532, he had visited Calais which led to 'A devyse made by the kinges highenes at his graces being at the town of Calis … for the fortificacion of the said towne', including gun embrasures 'made as the kinges grace hath devised'. Eight years later during work on the nearby fortification of Newneham Bridge west of Calais, the engineer Richard Lee noted that 'your Majesty hath devised the foresaid new tower'. In February 1539 when the work on the English coastal fortifications was just getting started, the plans for three bulwarks on the Downs were based on a 'device by the King' but this might be a reference to the overall construction program. Two months later, in a report describing the construction work on the fortification at East Cowes on the Isle of Wight, there is a comment that '170 persons work to finish it according to the platte devised by the King'.

Perhaps the words of his contemporaries sum up Henry's contribution. He was praised in 1539 for his constant concerns for the country's wellbeing, and for devising 'in tyme of warre, plattes, blocke howses, bulwarkes, walles, castelles … and fortresses'; while in 1546, he was described as 'a perfect builder as well of fortresses as of pleasant palaces'.

Sir Christopher Morris and James Nedeham

In his capacity as Master of the Ordnance, Morris was involved in the surveying of various fortresses including several on the Anglo-Scottish borders, which he described in January 1539 as quite appalling. His name appears in the original device scheme alongside that of James Nedeham as the 'master and devisers of the works' of the Thames bulwarks. Nedeham is identified in contemporary documents as clerk and surveyor of works, as well as a carpenter.

John Rogers and Richard Lee

Rogers, the master mason, and Lee, the surveyor of works, can be identified directly with the fortifications built at the English plantations of Guisnes and Calais in France, and possibly the works at Hull. Lee's name appears on a list of payments for 1541 as the surveyor of 'Calice' (Calais) and for constructing fortifications there. They were certainly aware of the new Italian-type bastioned fortification and introduced elements of

Plans of nine of Henry's castles.
1. Walmer. 2. Portland. 3. Camber (final phase). 4. Sandgate.
5. Pendennis. 6. Hurst. 7. Deal.
8. St Mawes. 9. Calshot.
(Andrew Saunders)

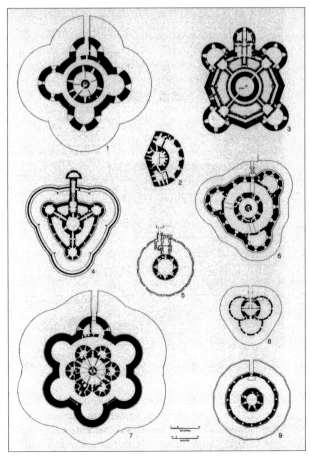

it at Hull and Guisnes, often in combination with the concentric designs of the earlier device forts. In 1544, Lee was in Portsmouth and might have been involved with the construction of Southsea Castle, and in the following year, during the French campaign against the Solent and the Isle of Wight, he was again in the town and might have had some influence on the design of Sandown Castle with its angle bastion.

Construction

Bulwarks, banks and ditches

It is clear that earthwork defences were constructed at several sites prior to the building of the masonry forts and later as corresponding fortifications. In fact, such 'bulwarks' may have outnumbered the masonry structures, but because they have not survived they have been generally overlooked. Nevertheless, it appears that earthwork fortifications formed a major part of the defensive scheme, and indeed the idea of revetted earthworks as a counter to heavy artillery had been developed earlier in France to support masonry fortifications.

At the outset, earthworks may have been a temporary measure to provide protection to the workers building the masonry forts from any attacks coming from France. For instance, at the sites of Calshot and Hurst castles in Hampshire protective structures of timber and hurdles filled with earth with sharpened stakes were erected immediately prior to construction of the masonry buildings. In August 1539, these earthen 'forts' were described by the French ambassador, Charles de Marillac, as 'not very durable, being made of stakes filled with earth as if made in a hurry', but they had clearly been designed as temporary stop-gap measures to counter the crisis of spring 1539 until the castles could be completed.

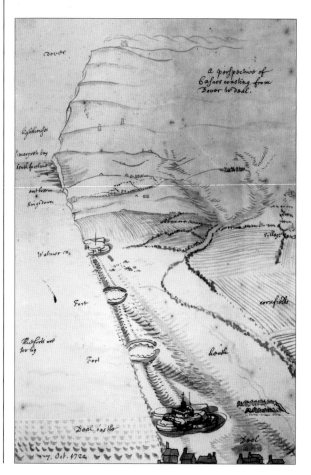

An aerial perspective of the earthwork defences in the Downs, drawn by William Stukeley in 1725. Deal Castle is in the foreground looking south towards Dover, Walmer is in the centre, while in between is the Great White Bulwark, with the Walmer Bulwark beyond. (SAL)

Other earthworks were hurriedly constructed at Portsmouth, East and West Cowes, and at Harwich on the Essex coast. On April 3, 1539, the Lord Chancellor, Thomas Audley, described in a letter to Cromwell the efforts of the local people to help in the construction: 'The Harwich people have been most willing and ernest, making both trenches and bulwarks before we came', and further on commented 'at Harwich ye should have seen women and children work with shovels in the trenches and bulwarks there'.

One location that was particularly vulnerable was the Downs, a deep-water area off the east coast of Kent north of Dover where there were good landing sites and shelter offered by the Goodwin Sands offshore. Hostile ships were frequently observed in the vicinity, so it was deemed vital to defend the adjacent coastline. In February 1539, steps were taken to improve the defences with a plan to construct three bulwarks. The result was the building of the three masonry castles at Sandown, Deal and Walmer. In addition were 'four bulwarks of earth in the Downs', most probably from designs supplied by Haschenperg. To the south of Sandown lay the Great Turf and Little Turf Bulwark; while between Deal and Walmer were the Great White Bulwark of Clay and the Walmer (or 'Blacke') Bulwark. All seven fortifications were apparently connected by a ditch or covered way stretching for the 2½ miles of coastline; and presumably there was a defensive exterior bank created from the quarrying of the ditch. They were designed to provide flanking arcs of fire to each other.

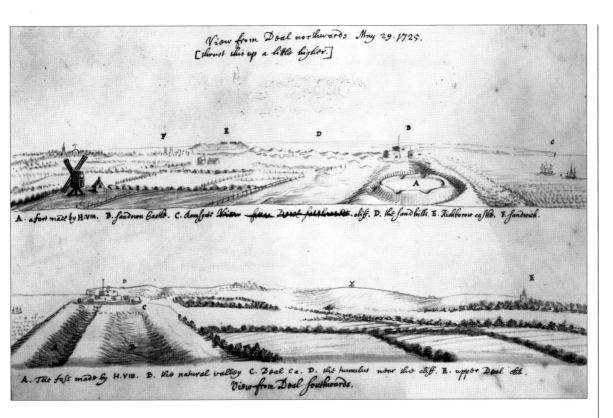

View from Deal northwards May 29. 1725.
[thrust this up a little higher.]

A. a fort made by H.VIII. B. sandown castle. C. Ramsgate ~~~~ cliff. D. the sandhills. E. Richborow castle. F. Sandwich.

A. The fort made by H.VIII. B. the natural valley C. Deal Ca. D. the tumulus near the cliff. E. upper Deal ch.
View from Deal southwards.

In Sir Christopher Morris's book of rates listing deliveries and payments to garrison commanders for 1539–40, other earthen forts are mentioned including 'the bulwark of earth upon the hill beyond the pier at Dover', and further bulwarks which may have been built of earth. It is probable that such temporary structures were constructed in concert with the permanent masonry fortifications as in the Downs.

Masonry castles and blockhouses
Accounts of the construction of the castles can be found in the *Letters and Papers, Foreign and Domestic of the Reign of Henry VIII*. On the Isle of Wight, for example, Thomas Canner, surveyor of the King's Works, visited the site of the two blockhouses under construction at Cowes in April 1539 and made this report:

> They find the foundation of the blockhouse at Est. Cowe digged and the wall brought up 4ft. above ground. Have set 170 persons to work to finish it according to the platte devised by the King. Their wages will amount to £113. 6s. 8d. a month. The carriage of stuff, taking down stone at the monasteries of Beaulieu and Quarre, &c., will amount to £160. a month. At West Cowe the expense will be the same. Total for both houses, £546. 13s. 4d. Can finish it by Michaelmas, or sooner with more men.
>
> Signed: Thomas Cannar, clerk – John Mowlton, masson – John Russell, carpenter.

On May 7, a letter from Robert Lorde, 'paymaster of parcel of the King's honourable works', to Thomas Cromwell written from Deal, Kent, describes the payment of 1,400 workmen with more expected to expedite the construction of the castles and fortifications in the Downs.

A document dated June 14, 1539 describes the situation at Gravesend on the north coast of Kent. It mentions payments made for the work on the

Another drawing by Stukeley. In the upper part, the Great White Bulwark is in the foreground with Sandown Castle beyond. In the lower part, the ditch and bank connecting the castles can be seen running towards Deal Castle. (SAL)

OPPOSITE **Sandgate Castle, Kent under construction, 1539–40**
This illustration shows the early stage of construction of a typical Henrician fort. Workers can be seen on the wooden scaffolding, while wagons full of masonry from a nearby demolished abbey are being unloaded. Stone was also quarried from the nearby coastline; boats were used for carrying the stone to the construction site. The construction workers are being supervised by Stephen von Haschenperg, seen on the centre right. Their accommodation tents can be seen in the distance.

blockhouse there and nearby: 'The workmen think that £3,000 more will finish all manner causes there ready begun'. A later estimate of charges, 'to be spent upon your Grace's fortress beside Gravesend from August [1539] to March [1540]', lists the following expenses: 14 masons at 8d. a day; 10 at 4d.; 12 labourers at 6d.; hard stone, £50 a month; a lodge for the masons to work in, £40; two lime-kilns and a lodge to hew the chalk in, £50; timber, £100; and Newcastle coal 'for to brine the lyme with,' £100. The cost of building one bulwark is estimated at £211 13s. 4d. which include 150,000 bricks, 200 tons of chalk, ashlar, timber, lime, workers and 'other necessaries'.

The most complete building account of any Tudor fortification survives in the two ledger books of payments for Sandgate Castle compiled by two commissioners, Thomas Cockys and Richard Keys; each page is also signed by Stefan de Haschenperg as noted above. Names of individual workers are indicated, as is the nature of their employment, such as carpenter, mason, carter or lime-burner. It describes costs, equipment, hours of work, and 'skavell men and rock breakers, digging and casting "beeche" from the foundation, breaking rocks and carrying them from the sea'. Materials were also brought in from the dissolved monastery of St Radegund's near Dover and from the Cluniac priory at Monks Horton six miles away.

Although the construction of the first group of castles was in full swing by April 1539, there were occasional setbacks and labour disputes as Cromwell found out in a letter from Sir Edward Ryngeley dated June 11, 1539:

> This week we had business with the King's labourers here [in the Downs], saying they would have 6d. a day, but after I had spoken with them I caused them to return work, as Robert Lord, who was present at Deal, can inform your Lordship. I have sent the 9 first beginners, 5 to Canterbury Castle, and 4 to Sandwych Gaol.

The first castles were functioning by the end of the year, and Deal was in a sufficient state to receive the king's future fourth wife, Anne of Cleves, who had landed there late in December 1539.

It is obvious that with the dissolution of so many abbeys and monasteries there was a ready supply of suitable stonework and lead, and most probably timber.

The Tudor blockhouse below St Mawes Castle, Cornwall. Like Pendennis, the first fortifications built at both sites consisted of semi-circular blockhouses near the water's edge. Originally roofed but later reduced in size, it had three gun-ports, a small fireplace and a water cistern. (PH)

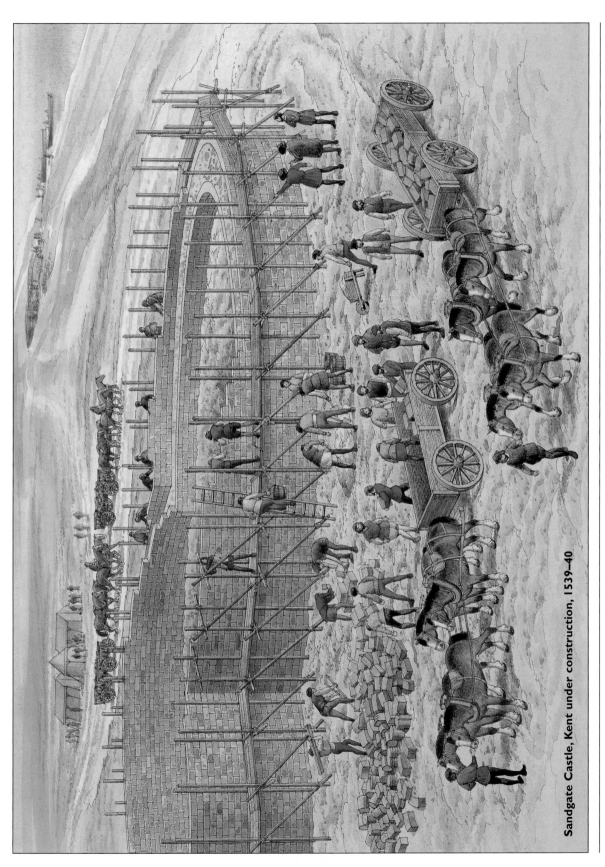

Sandgate Castle, Kent under construction, 1539–40

The principles of defence

The 1539 device programme

The first phase of the scheme saw the construction of 30 separate fortifications including ten significant 'castles' in their own right. These contain some elements clearly derived from the Continent, where the cylindrical tower was still the norm. Similar structures had been built earlier in England to guard harbour entrances at places such as Dover, Portsmouth and Dartmouth. At Dover, for example, the earliest pier had two stone towers built on it for defence, the outer one of which may have been constructed or remodelled around 1518 for it had more 'advanced' features such as rounded parapets and splayed gun-ports.

During the first phase of construction for the scheme, this curvilinear form was adapted and developed to create fortifications consisting of round artillery towers extending outwards into external round bastions for locating additional guns and housing for the garrison. These structures were squat with thick walls surmounted by parapets, and the walls were pierced with numerous square gun-ports splayed outwards. While the majority of the Phase 1 structures shared these characteristics, the fact that there were significant variations on their overall ground plans might suggest that they were designed by different military architects. Other factors such as availability of suitable building materials and local topography clearly came into play in determining the final designs.

Deal Castle (1539)

The largest of the three masonry forts built to protect the Downs, Deal was dominated by a strong central tower designed to serve as a gun platform, surrounded by six small semi-circular bastions. These smaller bastions were in turn situated upon six massive rounded and hollow bastions, the whole surrounded by a dry moat and a curtain wall. On the roofs of these large bastions were spaces for four guns to fire between the parapets or embrasures, while on the floors below were additional gun-ports. Each of these bastions was connected by a stretch of curtain wall bearing a further embrasure. In total, there was space for 66 guns arranged in four tiers. If an attacking force was able to penetrate into the dry moat, it would be met by the fire from 53 hand-guns firing through

BOTTOM LEFT An aerial view of Deal Castle on the south-east coast of Kent. This provides a clear indication of the symmetry of many of the Henrician fortifications. (PW)

BOTTOM RIGHT An aerial view of Walmer Castle in Kent. This lay at the southern end of a line of masonry and earthen fortified structures designed to protect the offshore anchorage of the Downs, and its arcs of fire were designed to overlap with those of Deal Castle to the north. (PW)

gun-loops arranged in a narrow gallery that ran around the basement level of the outer bastions. It was a self-contained fighting platform offering offensive as well as defensive capabilities.

Sandown and Walmer castles (1539)

While little remains of Sandown Castle, it appears to have been similar in form to its sister castles at Walmer and Deal. Both Walmer and Sandown were not as complex as Deal, however, but still possessed the same concentric forms with thick walls – however, a central circular tower was surrounded by four lower rounded bastions, rather than the six at Deal. Completing the arrangement was a dry moat surrounded by a curtain wall, with access to the structures via a drawbridge. Both castles had provision for three tiers of guns with a fourth tier in a basement gallery as at Deal for hand-gunners. There were, in all, 39 openings for large guns and 31 small loops for hand-guns. All three castles had double splays, casemates, smoke vents and ammunitions lockers.

Sandgate Castle (1539)

Unlike the other fortifications built during the defence programme, Sandgate was not sited to defend an anchorage or harbour. Rather, it was probably designed to defend against a landing along a vulnerable stretch of coastline between Dover and Folkestone. The proximity to the French coast only 25 miles away required it to be constantly defended and consequently Sandgate continued to serve as an important defensive site for several centuries. It went through a number of alterations and it is difficult to discern what form the original castle took. Sandgate was centrally planned to provide three lines of defence – an outer curtain, inner curtain and a keep. The three-storey keep surmounted by rounded parapets was surrounded by the two concentric curtains, the outer one around a ward or barbican, and an inner curtain containing three round towers equidistant around the keep and connected by corresponding radiating wings. A gatehouse, also three storeys high, was located within a fourth wing. The castle was designed so that the structure rose progressively from the outer curtain to the keep providing three or four tiers of heavy guns positioned behind 65 gun-ports or well-splayed embrasures. Gun-loops in the lowest level of the two-storey round towers protected the barbican, and further loops were situated on the inner walls of the round towers and wings. In all, there were 130 possible gun positions.

Camber Castle (1539)

Based on an existing round tower built between 1512 and 1514 to protect the harbour of Rye in Sussex, the new Henrician castle that was completed in 1540 went through a second major modification in 1542–43. In keeping with the

BOTTOM LEFT The ruins of Camber Castle, Sussex, situated near the towns of Rye and Winchelsea. The present design reflects three building phases commencing with a circular keep sometime after 1512. (PW)

BOTTOM RIGHT An engraving after a painting by J. M. W. Turner showing the dark silhouette of Camber Castle on the levels below the market town of Rye, Sussex. Within a few decades of its construction, the sea had begun to recede leaving the castle away from the coast. (ASKB)

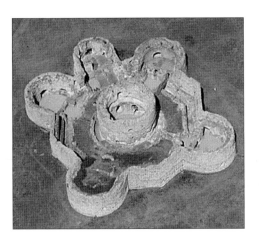

OPPOSITE **Walmer, Deal and Sandown castles**

An elevated view looking northwards of the 'Castles in the Downs' along the east coast of Kent, showing Walmer, Deal and Sandown as they appeared in the early 1540s, and the way they were connected by earthworks and earthen forts. This illustration is based on the contemporary painting currently hanging in Walmer Castle. Walmer is in the right foreground, Deal is in the middle distance, and beyond lies Sandown. Between Walmer and Deal lie the circular earthworks of the Walmer Bulwark and the Great White Bulwark. The area was a critical anchorage for ships. The castles worked in concert with each other to provide overlapping arcs of fire.

standard design, the structure had at its centre a circular keep that was built upon the original tower. This was surrounded by an elaborate concentric system of four bastions. These in turn were backed by four D-shaped towers linked to each other by an octagonal curtain. A massive rectangular gatehouse completed the fortification, which presented a low profile and was surrounded by an earthwork glacis. The perimeter was commanded by flankers concealed in the bastions, but as the bastions were rounded, there was still dead ground. However, Camber has been described as an early attempt by von Haschenperg to build an artillery fortification in England inspired by Italian ideas, particularly the low profile, flankers and the external glacis. Nonetheless, two years later the four bastions were replaced by four massive semi-circular bastions connected by an eight-sided curtain. This modification created a fortification that was higher than the previous one. In effect this rebuilding with its increased height and massive rounded bastions was more archaic than its predecessor.

Portland and Sandsfoot castles (1539)

The defence of the Dorset coast was viewed as an essential component of the overall device project, and the towns of Weymouth and Portland were earmarked for new fortifications to guard the vital anchorage of Portland Roads. Work commenced on 'Portland bulwark' in summer 1539 and it was ready by the end of the following year. The result was very different to its sister castles, being one of the smallest of the group and resembling a segment of a circle. While it has a central keep, its defensive posture is solely coastal facing and it lacks all-round defence. Its outer segmental gun platform does not surround the keep. Nonetheless, the geometrical plan places it with those at Deal, Walmer, Sandown, Hurst and St Mawes. Sandsfoot, in contrast, was a two-storey rectangular structure behind a five-sided gun platform overlooking the sea.

Portland Castle, Dorset, situated on the water's edge, was constructed between 1539 and 1540 to protect the vital anchorage of 'Portland Roads'. It is in the form of a segment of a circle, consisting of a central two-storey keep flanked by rectangular wings on each side. (PL)

22

Walmer, Deal and Sandown castles

TOP LEFT Pendennis Castle, situated opposite St Mawes, is quite different in layout. The original castle consisted of a central circular tower surrounded by a low, multi-sided 'chemise' or gun platform, but later additions have changed the overall appearance of the site. (PH)

TOP RIGHT St Mawes Castle, Cornwall, was built to protect the eastern shore of the River Fal. The castle presents a fine clover-leaf shape and, unlike many of its sister castles, the walls are adorned with symbols of the monarch. (PH)

BOTTOM LEFT Calshot Castle, Hampshire, was built at the end of a short spit to command the entrance to Southampton Water. It shares similarities with Pendennis with a circular keep surrounded by a low 16-sided curtain wall. The gatehouse range is a later alteration of the original entrance. (SW)

BOTTOM RIGHT The curtain wall at Calshot was originally much higher with 15 embrasures, but was lowered in the 18th century, possibly to allow a better field of fire from the keep. The concrete searchlight emplacement built in the 1890s can be seen just above the curtain wall and the moat. (SW)

Pendennis and St Mawes castles (1540)

At both sites are small semi-circular blockhouses situated close to the water's edge, commanding the mouth of the River Fal at Falmouth, Cornwall. It appears that these were built just prior to the device programme in 1538 and may have been temporary defences until the main castles could be built. They are similar to Bayard's Cove at Dartmouth, and other blockhouses built around the coast. The one below St Mawes has three gun-ports piercing the thick walls supporting a roof that served as a platform for additional guns, but there were also facilities for a small garrison consisting of a fireplace, oven and water cistern.

In 1540, work began on both headlands adjacent to the river to construct solid circular structures for mounting guns, but the results were quite different. Whereas St Mawes was built below the headland and its design elements are more in keeping with the other Phase 1 castles, Pendennis (atop a promontory) has only a central tower, 57ft in diameter, surrounded by a very low circular curtain wall or chemise. This and an elaborate gatehouse containing the commander's apartments were most probably added later, while a massive bastioned enceinte was constructed in the Elizabethan period. The tower had guns on two floors and on the roof.

St Mawes, in contrast, is perfectly geometric in plan. A central tower 46ft in diameter stands four storeys high – if one includes a small turret with cupola. The whole rises 44ft from base to parapet. Around this are three low, semi-circular bastions arranged in a clover-leaf pattern. Each bastion has embrasures at ground level to accommodate large cannon, while additional guns were sited on the roof of the tower and bastions.

Calshot Castle (1540)

Located on a piece of shingle beach jutting into the mouth of the strategic Southampton Water where it meets the Solent, Calshot bears the closest resemblance to Pendennis. Simple in design but centrally planned, it was begun in 1539 and completed the following year, and consists of a three-storey

Hurst Castle in the 18th century with the Needles Passage and the Isle of Wight in the background. It was considered one of the most sophisticated of the castles, and was designed primarily to stop enemy shipping from entering the western end of the Solent. (ASKB)

central tower or keep surrounded by a low concentric curtain wall and a stone-lined moat, but with no extra-mural bastions. Arranged in three tiers on the keep roof, on the second floor of the keep (and possibly the first floor) and in the curtain wall were eight embrasures and 18 gun-ports. An additional space for three guns on the gatehouse served as a defence against an attack along the spit on which the castle was built. The gun platforms at Calshot were clad with lead removed from nearby Beaulieu Abbey.

Hurst Castle (1541)

Although not mentioned in the original scheme, and of later construction, Hurst was far more advanced than the other castles built in the first phase, with its numerous firing levels, its flankers and the layout of the ground-level casemates. Constructed between 1541 and 1544 on the coast of Hampshire just across the water from the site of an early fortification known as Worsley's Tower (c.1520–38), Hurst commanded the critical Needles Passage at the western entrance to the Solent and could observe any shipping entering the seaway. Situated on a low, shingle spit that jutted into the sea only 1,400 yards from the Isle of Wight, the castle was designed to withstand attack from the sea as well as land, with embrasures for over 70 weapons. Although it was not completed until 1544, its overall plan mirrored the earlier forts with their emphasis on curvilinear features. Somewhat similar in design to Sandgate, it was, nonetheless, one of the most sophisticated of the castles built up to this point. A twelve-sided tower was surrounded by a similar geometric curtain wall linking three projecting semi-circular bastions, all originally surrounded by a moat crossed by a bridge. The three building levels consisted of a basement below a ground floor on the same level as the surrounding shingle beach, surmounted by a first floor which is on the same level as the parapet of two of the three bastions. The parapets of the third bastion adjacent to the gate and of the keep are higher still. In all, the castle had six tiers with 71 gun-ports or embrasures, six flankers at moat level, and 18 casemates on the ground level.

Hurst consisted originally of a large 12-sided keep, with a basement, two floors and a roof bearing the distinctive curved parapets. In the 19th century, the roof and parapets of the keep were altered considerably. (SW)

St Mawes Castle, Cornwall

This shows a typical Henrician castle upon completion and in use, with cutaway views of the interior of the main tower and front bastion.

1 Ditch encircling the entire castle (this was filled in later).
2 The main tower, with the roof being used as a gun platform.
3 Top internal floor, combined gun and barrack room (hand-guns only).
4 Garrison mess room (main living area) partitioned into smaller rooms.
5 Basement kitchen, subdivided (the larger room contains fireplace, with a brick-lined bread oven built into it, and a granite pedestal table).
6 The forward gun room of the front bastion. Each alcove or 'casemate' has a smoke vent and sockets for a beam that would have held a wooden shutter.
7 and 8 The side bastions, with guns on top.
9 The entrance and blockhouse.

The rear of the north-west bastion of Hurst Castle. A narrow courtyard separates the keep from three substantial semi-circular bastions. As it covered the gateway and the land approach, this bastion was the most powerful of the three. (SW)

There were 11 embrasures in the curtain parapet with an additional ten arranged in the two lower bastions, and six in the third higher bastion. In the keep were eight gun-ports on the same level as the parapets of the two lower bastions, and 12 embrasures on the roof.

Other sites

A number of other forts dated from Phase 1 of the device, among them East Cowes and West Cowes and St Andrew's Castle, and those around the Thames estuary. The River Medina flows due north from the centre of the Isle of Wight where it meets the Solent at Cowes. Two small blockhouses were built on each side of the mouth. On the east bank, a small fort was built, but little is known of its layout. It was probably similar in design to that at West Cowes. The latter consisted of a two-storey central round tower with flanking rectangular wings, one storey high on the east and west side, surrounded on the seaward side by a semi-circular curtain. Facing inland, the fort was protected by a walled ditch. Guns were located on the roof of the tower and the wings, and around the circular curtain so that they were situated in three tiers.

Five bulwarks or blockhouses were built around the Thames estuary: at Gravesend, at Milton 503m to the east, and across the river at Tilbury; and further east on the north (Essex) shore at East Tilbury, and on the south (Kent) shore at Higham. Little remains of these sites although excavations have revealed some details. Most appear to have a D-shaped plan and some may have had surrounding earthworks. All five were complete and operational by 1540 and the largest, at Milton, mounted 30 guns and six hand-guns, as well as bows and pikes. Gravesend, Milton and Tilbury crossed their fire with each other, as did East Tilbury and Higham.

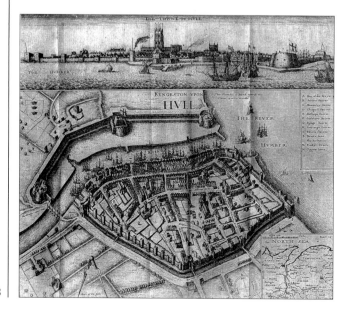

A 17th-century plan showing the defences of Hull, on the River Humber, Yorkshire, including three bulwarks connected by a crenellated wall situated to the north of the port beyond the River Hull. (ASKB)

West Cowes Castle, Isle of Wight, as depicted in an 18th-century engraving. It was constructed to work in unison with its sister fort at East Cowes, and both were considerably smaller than many of the other Henrician castles. (ASKB)

Work was also carried out at Hull in 1542 to re-fortify the town and port. It had first been earmarked for fortification in the original device scheme of 1539 but was passed over in favour of the south coast. This belated work resulted from a visit by the king and followed his 'device'. It consisted of a defensive line anchored on a central strong point with two hollow, multi-storeyed bastions, connected by a crenellated wall nearly half a mile long with two bulwarks or blockhouses at each end. These three forts would present a defence against an overland attack from the east or a seaborne attack from the adjacent river.

Finally, mention should be made of Calais and Guisnes. English possessions since the Hundred Years' War, they were considered vital to defend, especially Calais situated at the narrowest point of the English Channel. Both were included in the original device scheme of early 1539, and work continued on and off throughout Henry's reign to strengthen the fortifications and construct new bastions and bulwarks.

The 1544 device programme

The threat of 1539 passed as quickly as it came, and by the time most of the earlier castles had come online, any fear of an invasion from the Continent had abated. A new war with France broke out, however, in the 1540s and the construction scheme was renewed, especially around the vulnerable Solent

A detail from the 17th-century plan of Hull showing the eastern bulwark connected by a defensive line to another. Note the semi-circular walls, the curved embrasures and the gun-ports. This is in contrast to the central bulwark, which is rectilinear. (ASKB)

Southsea Castle, Hampshire, one of the later Henrician castles and reflective of new ideas in fortification. Here, circularity has been dispensed with, to be replaced by angular walls. Its appearance today is quite different from that of the original Tudor castle. (SW)

estuary and the vital ports of Southampton and Portsmouth. However, the forts built during the second phase began to reflect new ideas about fortification and took on more angular appearances reflecting principles then being adapted on the Continent. Round towers and curved bastions were gradually replaced with square keeps and angular bastions.

Southsea Castle (1544)

As late as the 20th century, the Solent was considered a vital passage for ships leaving Portsmouth and Southampton. In the 1540s, this region was vulnerable to attack from the French and its defence was critical to national interests. Just as Hurst Castle was located to guard the west entrance, Calshot at the north end where it entered Southampton Water, and the blockhouses protected Cowes, the approaches to the eastern passage had to be defended, particularly the entrance to Portsmouth harbour. At the mouth of this deep-water channel where ships passed close to the shore, a castle was built on the southern point of Portsea Island at Southsea, but unlike its predecessors everything about the place was square and angular rather than round and curved. The structure had a square keep and on the east and west were rectangular gun platforms. More significant were the angular bastions on the north and south. Near the foot of the curtain wall were eight gun openings or flankers to oppose any attackers who got into the dry moat.

Sandown Castle (1545)

In the same way, the south-east coast of the Isle of Wight overlooking Sandown Bay was chosen for another fort in expectation of a French attack – which did materialize in the summer of 1545. That it was completed within five months

OPPOSITE **Southsea Castle, Hampshire, c.1545**
Southsea Castle was in marked contrast to the first phase in Henrician fortification. The earlier circular forts gave way to angular, square forts. The castle has a square central keep, two rectangular gun platforms, and two angular bastions. There is also a dry moat with a drawbridge across it. Ships can be seen in the Solent beyond the castle, and wagons are arriving with fresh supplies for the garrison. The Isle of Wight can be seen in the distance. The central keep as it appears today has been much reduced in height.

1 and **2** Gun platforms
3 Central keep
4 and **5** Angled bastions
6 Gate and drawbridge
7 Dry moat
8 Flankers (gun openings near foot of wall)
9 Guardhouses

Southsea Castle, Hampshire, c.1545

suggests that it was modest in scale, consisting of a walled courtyard dominated by a square keep with two bastions and a moat on the landward side, and a semi-circular bastion overlooking the bay. What sets Sandown apart from the earlier Henrician castles are the two bastions, which were rectilinear rather than semi-circular and flanked the three landward sides of the fort, although neither had recessed flankers like the later structure at Yarmouth. The western bastion was a rectangle projecting into the moat flanking the curtain walls to the north-west and south-west. In the same way, the north bastion flanked the adjacent curtains but unlike its counterpart, was angular. This true angled bastion may have represented one of the earliest attempts to embrace Italian principles of fortification developed in the late 15th century.

Yarmouth Castle (1547)

The Henrician style of fortification had become obsolete around the mid 1540s especially with the introduction of the Italian style based on the angled bastion, ravelins and other new features. The last castle completed as part of the coastal defence scheme, at Yarmouth, therefore embodied the most up-to-date features of military engineering, and stands in stark contrast to its predecessors of 1539–40. Concentric design was out. Now everything was square and angular. The triangular-shaped bastion that would come to dominate fortification around the world well into the 19th century had now been adopted in England, and it made an early appearance at Yarmouth. Unlike many of the earlier forts, Yarmouth consisted of a square, walled enclosure protected on the two landward sides by a ditch, while a two-storey angular bastion with recessed flankers jutted out from the south-east corner to cover the ditch and curtains on the east and south sides. Nevertheless, the castle was somewhat of an anomaly, possibly reflecting the uncertainty about the new designs of the English engineers. The faces of the bastion were completely unprotected suggesting an ignorance of the concept of supporting fire. Furthermore, the walls of the structure were rather high, and lacking any earth backing to absorb impact they were vulnerable to bombardment.

Other sites

Some fortifications were sponsored primarily by private groups or individuals. Netley Castle, further up Southampton Water from Calshot, was constructed in 1542 in the grounds of the recently dissolved abbey by Lord St John, who had received the property from the king. Although early for castles of the second phase, it is closer in style to them because of its angular construction. It consisted of a single-storey rectangular building 19.5m wide by 14m deep with gun platforms on each side. The roof of the main building had four widely splayed embrasures facing the water.

The final castle of Henry's reign was built at Yarmouth on the north-west coast of the Isle of Wight. It stands in marked contrast to the curvilinear castles of 1539–40, with its diamond-shaped bastion attached to a rectangular structure. (SW)

A view of the east side of Yarmouth Castle showing the two-storey angled bastion on the left, flanking the original entrance which lies between the two privet hedges. Above the entrance are the original royal arms. (SW)

Similarly, a small blockhouse was built on Brownsea Island near Poole, Dorset, at the expense of the town and the king. It dated from between 1545 and 1547, but only the lower storey of a planned two-storey building was completed. A hexagonal wall projected from the rectangular block towards the sea enclosing a gun platform. The roof of the main building also served as a gun platform.

Some of the structures from the 1539 device may have been modified during this period, such as the addition of an angular bastion to the Milton blockhouse, possibly in 1545. Major ports such as Portsmouth were also re-fortified. The works at Portsmouth constructed between 1545 and 1546 were supervised by Sir Richard Lee.

Across the Needles Passage from Hurst Castle and about 800 yards north-east from Worsley's Tower, a bulwark was constructed on Sconce Point between August 1545 and December 1547. Sharpenrode Bulwark, as it was known, was constructed following the French attack on the Solent, and was designed to control the Needles Passage and support the guns at Hurst. A contemporary document describes the fortification:

> yt is a massy platform only walled wyth planke ... wythout anny dytche aboute yt. This bulwerk ys about xxxvii fote square and viii fote high to the see wardes, and hath two flankers wyth a hier wall to the landewardes, wherby they may flanker the pece with hercubusses that elles might beate them from the hill at ther backes.

It was one of the earliest sites in Britain to employ fortifications reflecting the new Italian style, namely the angle bastion, referred to as flankers in the preceding account.

With the exception of Camber, which soon outgrew its value, all the masonry castles constructed between 1539 and 1547 did not remain static structures for long but were continuously added to over the succeeding centuries. As they were situated in locations that remained strategically important well into the 20th century, they went through many building phases to keep them militarily current, so much so that today it is often difficult to identify the original Tudor structures of Henry's programme at several sites such as Sandgate, Netley and Hurst.

Yarmouth Castle, Isle of Wight, 1547

34

A tour of the sites

Although the first- and second-phase castles differ in overall plan, they do share what has been termed a 'Henrician style'. These common characteristics include a central tower or keep, either round or square, surrounded by concentric or symmetric external hollow, roofed bastions, whether curvilinear or angled. Sometimes these were connected directly to the main keep or separated by open space. Anyone visiting these structures between 1539 and 1546 would have been impressed with their low-lying, squat appearance in contrast to the towering bulks of medieval castles that were so familiar around England. From ground level, the walls would have risen tier by tier towards the keep, offering three to five levels for artillery.

Approaching the entrance of one of the new castles would require traversing a moat or dry ditch, if the land permitted them, usually by means of a wooden bridge that could be drawn up in times of crisis. Looking at the surrounding walls, a series of tiered gun-ports would provide an obvious difference to medieval fortifications. These ports would have wide external splays allowing guns to traverse a broad field of fire. Across the bridge, the visitor would pass under a traditional portcullis and murder holes to the guardhouse, which would be located in the outer bastioned defences. These rounded or angular bastions were generally open at the gorge, which would have prevented them from being used by attackers against the garrison. The bastions were floored across for mounting two tiers of guns; later some of the hollow bastions were filled with earth to create solid platforms. Upon passing through the outer defences, the thickness of the masonry walls, from three to five metres, would be striking, and there might be holes in the roof to vent smoke from the guns. Once through the outer perimeter, another open space or courtyard would present itself at several of the sites, and the main tower would be ahead and central to the structure. The curved walls and parapets would present symmetry, all designed to deflect projectiles.

The gatehouse of Deal formed in the western outer bastion would have had a drawbridge, but is now accessed via a stone causeway. The original upper storey was removed later. Inside are the remains of the portcullis grooves. (PW)

OPPOSITE **Yarmouth Castle, Isle of Wight, 1547**
This illustration shows Yarmouth Castle on the north-west coast of the Isle of Wight shortly after completion in 1547. Like Southsea, it demonstrates the advances in fortification principles from the earlier forts, especially in the presence of an angular bastion jutting out from the south-east corner of the main square building. The castle was built on low ground, probably reclaimed land. The main building consists of three floors, with the parapet level (comprising a timber platform) splayed with four embrasures on each wall. The north and west sides of the castle rose straight from the foreshore, while the other sides faced the town, hence the need for the angular bastion to defend this area. The landward side of the castle was also protected by a 30ft-wide ditch.

One of the side bastions or 'lunettes' at St Mawes, showing the casemates for heavy guns. This would have been originally roofed to allow additional guns to be mounted. Note the thickness of the wall, a common feature of all the Henrician forts. (PH)

Inside the central keep accommodation rooms would be located, although sometimes these were found in the outer bastions due to inadequate space in the keep. Internal wooden partitions divided the rooms up, creating dark and cramped living quarters. Storage would be in the basement, with the ground floor reserved for a common mess hall; the kitchens would also be found on this floor and possibly soldiers' quarters. Officers' quarters, including the captain's, would be situated on the upper floors.

Obviously, a different situation would present itself at the earthwork bulwarks, where accommodation would be spartan to say the least. As none have survived, it is difficult to know exactly what the internal arrangements were. There may have been small timber buildings to house the garrison, although it is just as likely that the garrisons lived elsewhere beyond the earthworks.

The living sites

By the end of December 1540, 24 new fortifications had been completed and garrisoned, but by then the threat of invasion from the Continent had evaporated. Thereafter, life in these artillery forts both large and small was, for the most part, uneventful, and the soldiers must have viewed themselves as living in isolated outposts largely ignored by their government in London. This is in sharp contrast to the times of emergency, especially in the mid 1540s, when the country was faced with invasion on several occasions, and later in the century during the war with Spain. It was in these times of national crisis that the castles must have been the very picture of intense activity. The buildings would have come alive with the hustle and bustle of humanity as the garrisons swelled with the arrival of soldiers and volunteers from the surrounding countryside, and weapons and munitions were re-supplied. In and around the fortifications, soldiers drilled and gunners conducted target practice. Meanwhile, local purveyors would have been arriving at the castles with wagons loaded with food and other provisions. Beacons were prepared in anticipation of the very real possibility of invasion. The historical documents reveal a major concern about likely landing places along the south coast of England and the need for increased vigilance. No doubt, additional earthwork defences were hastily thrown up along the cliff tops and shoreline to work in concert with the masonry forts.

Garrisons

Once complete, these massively built castles were 'completely self-contained unit[s] of warfare equipped with a bewildering array of access arrangements', as one writer described the way Camber would have appeared in 1543. Nevertheless, the fortifications were defended by relatively small 'holding' garrisons, who would have provided little more than care and maintenance for the guns.

There are no descriptions of the daily routine of the men living in these self-contained fortifications. The only details come from books of payments for wages, and accounts listing names of the commanders and numbers of soldiers.

A mannequin on display at St Mawes representing one of the garrison armed with a hand-gun. Life for them must have been tedious except at times of emergency, such as the French war of 1545 and the Spanish war of the late 16th century. (PH)

For instance, a captain was paid between 12d and 24d per day, a porter between 6d and 8d, and gunners each received a daily rate of 6d. In one document dated December 31, 1540, names of some of the men serving in the various garrisons are given. For example, at Calshot Castle, the following soldiers' names are listed: 'Wm. Shirland, c[aptain]., Ralph King, p[orter]., Roger Walton, Roger Mariner, Wm. Hare, Ric. Woton, Hen. Ball, Edm. Stanton, Oswald Danges, and Robt. Baites'. Another document suggests that besides the captain, there were 12 gunners based at Calshot. At one of the blockhouses on the Thames, the garrison consisted of a captain, a deputy, a porter, two soldiers and six gunners; while at Deal there were 34 men under the command of one captain.

One book of payments bearing the date of January 15, 1541 and compiled by Edward North, the Treasurer of Augmentations, provides the following information that relates particularly to the small bulwarks and earthen fortifications:

Bulwark at Gravesend: – Payment, 6 Jan … to Jas. Crane, captain, 1 porter and 5 gunners. Mylton: – 6 Jan., Sir Edw. Cobham, captain, 1 porter and 5 gunners. Over against Gravesend: 6 Jan., Fras. Graunte, captain, &c., Tylbery: – 6 Jan., Hugh Boyvyle, captain, &c. Hygham, Kent: – 6 Jan., John Yardley, captain, &c. Castle at Sandhyll next to Sandwyche: – 11 Jan., Ric. Deryng, captain, Walter Sooley, deputy, &c. Bulwark of turf next Sandhyll Castle, and the little bulwark of turf: – 3 and 2 gunners respectively. The Great Castle at Deale: – 11 Jan., Thos. Wyngfyld, captain, Robt. Roffe, deputy, &c. The Great white bulwark of clay: – 11 Jan., 4 gunners. The bulwark of turf next to Walmer Castle: – 4 gunners. Walmer Castle: – 11 Jan., Thos. Allyn, captain, John Barley, deputy, &c. Bulwark under Dover Castle: – 12 Jan., Thos. Vaughan, captain, &c. Under the cliff going to the Wyke [Dover]: – Robt. Nethersall, captain, &c. Upon the hill beyond the pier: – Edm. Mody, captain, &c. Folston [Folkstone] castle: – 14 Jan., Ric. Keys, captain, Jas. Starkey, deputy, &c. The castle of the Camber upon the Cabell Poynt: – 14 Jan., Ph. Chewt, captain, &c. Town of Rye: – 15 Jan., one gunner. Total pay for each place signed by Antony and Gold.

A mannequin at St Mawes positioned by a gun-port alongside a small cannon mounted on a stock. Besides firearms, the garrisons of many of the castles were equipped with more archaic weapons such as bows, hooks, scythes and halberds. (PH)

A similar document compiled in the previous year by the Master of Ordnance Sir Christopher Morris gives the numbers of men garrisoning all the bulwarks and castles, amounting to 2,220 individuals at a cost of £2,208 8s 0d a year.

Besides providing names of the captains, these documents and others like them are also informative as to the location and types of fortifications constructed or refurbished during the programme, many of which have not survived. In particular, Dover appears to have had a number of earthwork fortifications situated above and around the harbour.

The task of the soldiers garrisoning the castles was keeping the weapons in a reasonable state of working order, making sure that there were adequate supplies of ammunition and stores, and looking after the fabric of the castle. They probably also conducted target practice and gun drills. Generally, however, they served as caretakers.

Life in the forts

Accommodation in many of the new fortifications would have been very simple and designed for a small permanent garrison with sleeping quarters, a mess room and garderobes. Water was obtained from wells, with fireplaces providing heat and cooking spaces. While the external walls and parapets supported the weapons, the rest of the structures incorporated the living space.

This was divided up by timber-framed partitions and the upper part of the main keeps was given over to the captain's quarters. At Camber, garderobes and fireplaces were constructed in the third-phase renovations of 1542–43 in the entrance bastion and curtain wall galleries. Other improvements included glazed windows and heating facilities. A total of seven garderobes were added, which was more than enough for the small garrison. These may have been built in anticipation of the need to augment the permanent garrison during times of emergency. The fact that there were no garderobes in the central keep, only fireplaces, suggests that this part of the fort was not used for sleeping.

Based on the archaeological evidence from Camber, it has been suggested that the diet of the garrison was adequate but not luxurious. Meat and fish were consumed and the soldiers might have supplemented their food by catching, trapping and fishing. Beef was the main source of meat, but the animal bones recovered indicate the low status of the gunners and soldiers. Small amounts of bones from turkey, peafowl, deer and turbot – considered signatures of a higher status – suggest that these animals were consumed only on rare occasions, possibly during visits to the castle by high-ranking officers. Dogs were present and may have been used for guard duties or as mascots, while cats were brought in to control mice and rats. The situation at Camber was not unique and might reflect similar practices throughout the general fortification system.

Rules and regulations

Strict rules establishing a code of discipline were set down in 1539 for the governance of garrisons. In the *Ordinances and Statutes Devised by the King's Majesty for the Rule, Establishment, and Surety of his Highness's Castles, Bulwarks, and Other Fortresses Appointed to the Survey of the Lord Admiral*, the following regulations were laid out:

1. The captain of a castle must not be absent more than eight nights in a month without special licence from the king, on pain of forfeiting wages.
2. The deputy was not to be absent more than four nights a month, and never when the captain was away, under similar penalties.
3. Nor the porters more than three nights, and when absent must find a substitute.
4. Every day certain of the gunners and soldiers must keep guard, the numbers to be determined by the Admiral. Absentees must find a substitute.
5. Two gunners and soldiers were to keep watch every night, and if found sleeping or absent from their circuit, to forfeit two days' wages for the first offence.
6. The captain or deputy, with the whole ward for the day, must be present daily at the opening of the gates, morning, noon and night. The gates of the castles were to be opened and shut on a regulated schedule according to the season of the year and hours of daylight.
7. No strangers were to be admitted, nor any group numbering more than half the garrison.
8. Captains were not allowed to exact payment from ships in transit at anchor.
9. Garrisons were not allowed to indulge in hunting wild game.
10. Soldiers had to furnish their own weapons, particularly a hand-gun or 'hagbush'. Failure to do so could result in the forfeiture of three days' wages.
11. Unless commanded by the captain, no gunner was to shoot off ordnance or summon any ship, on pain of losing his place.
12. Any law suits against members of the garrison had to be made to the lord Admiral.
13. Any food taken by members of the garrison must be declared before wages were paid.

A gun-loop for hand-guns in one of the semi-circular bastions at St Mawes. This is adjacent to a casemate for heavy guns. The garrisons were armed with an array of small weapons available in the event of an attack from land. (PH)

14. Captains must never allow more than two soldiers to be absent at any one time.
15. Allowances of powder for exercise, and for 'halsing [saluting] of ships, and trying of pieces' would be made at the Lord Admiral's discretion.
16. Each of the captains, deputies, gunners and porters were to have their bills signed by the king.
17. Quarterly musters were to be taken and each man must take an oath that the orders were to be kept.
18. Inventories of munitions were taken at the first muster, and must be reviewed every quarter.
19. Death certificates of any of the garrison must be made to the Lord Admiral.
20. No soldier must leave or be discharged, except at musters, or by permission in writing from the Lord Admiral.
21. Any man 'making an affray' at the gates, or on the walls, or at night, would lose his place and be imprisoned.
22. Failure to keep the oath would result in imprisonment for disobedience, and other penalties.

The oath that every member of the garrison had to swear was as follows:

To be true and faithful to Henry the Eighth, and to his heirs according to the statute in the 27th year of his reign; to disclose anything heard prejudicial to the King, the realm, or this fortress; to observe the rules of the fortress, and disclose any violation of them at the next musters; to be no 'quarrell picker', and disclose any contention in the retinue; to be obedient to the lord Admiral, captain, or deputy.

Life in the castles must have been tedious and tensions between the garrisons might have occasionally been high. For example, on November 18, 1545 the Privy Council in London received the following complaint:

John Barley, deputy of Walmer castle, complaining of interruption by Wm. Blechenden, his captain, and John Barrowe and Henry Griffyn, gunners there, complaining that they are thrust out, letters were written to Blechenden for their continuance.

In April the following year, the Privy Council issued warrants to the treasurer of the Chamber for 38 shillings, for conduct and coats, 'to John Barroe [sic] and Henry Griffyn, late gunners at Walmer castle and dismissed for lewd demeanour to their captain'.

Weaponry

All the castles and fortifications built during the 'device' scheme were essentially self-contained platforms for mounting heavy artillery, and accommodation for the attendant gun crews and their commanders; parts of the structures were also designed for small arms to fend off any attackers who managed to penetrate the outer defences. The king himself took a keen interest in firepower and actively encouraged the design of new ordnance. An example was his efforts to find a cheaper and faster method of constructing guns, and his plans to bring together craftsmen and ironworkers for experiments at a Sussex ironworks resulted in a method for an improved and safer method of casting iron guns.

A visit to the new castles at the time would have revealed a variety of weapons surmounting the circular keeps as well as within the adjoining bastions; the associated earthwork fortifications would have also provided protection for heavy ordnance. The guns would have covered both seaward and landward approaches. Constructed from brass and iron, the artillery came in a variety of sizes as well as a variety of names such as culverins, falcons, sakers, minions, cannon and demi-cannon. The size determined the calibre of the solid shot and the range of the weapons. For instance, a demi-cannon fired a 32 lb. shot, in contrast to a saker that fired a round shot weighing 6 lb. The largest could fire a shot up to 1,000m. All were mounted on wooden gun carriages for ease of movement.

The typical hand-gun of the period was the arquebus, an early form of musket five or six feet in length supported by a tripod. It was fired by a matchlock device.

A surviving inventory dating from 1547–48 provides details of guns and munitions in all the royal castles. It was compiled from surveys taken at each castle between December 20, 1547 and March 3, 1548, and is highly informative as to the various weapons housed in each of the Henrician forts. Twenty-eight different types of guns (besides hand-guns) are listed including bombards, double cannon, cannon, sakers, minions, robinets, slings and mortars. In the majority of the fortifications, slings, bases, fowlers and small-calibre guns were the most common ordnance employed. At 17 forts built or expanded during Henry's reign, demi-cannon with a 6.5in. calibre were mounted. The main guns used included both muzzle-loading and breech-loading varieties, and the inventory listed everything including crowbars, sledges and gynnes with brass pulley blocks for mounting ordnance. One example, that of St Mawes Castle in Cornwall, will provide some idea of the range of armament that could be found in a typical castle during the late 1540s:

> Saint Mawse in Falmouth in the Countie of Cornwall. Ordenaunce artillery and other munycions or habillentes of warr remayning in the said Fortresse in the charge of Thomas Treffrey Captayne of the same the xxvj day of December Annon Regni Regis Edwardi vj nunc primo.

Demy Cannon   oone
Demy Culveryne   oone
Port pieces mounted wt viij chambers   iiij[or]
Slinges mounted wt ixen Chambers   v[e]
Demy slinges   oone
Basses mounted wt xvj chambers   vij[en]
Hagbusshes   xij[e]
Demy Cannon and di' Culveryne shot of yron   iiij[xx] xiiij[en]
Shotte of stone for porte pieces   Cxxvij[ti]
Slinge shot of leade diced wt stone and yron   CC
Demy sling shott of lead diced wt stone and yrone   xl[ti]
Shot of leade dyced wt stone and yrone for bases   CC
Shot for hagbusshes of leade diced wt stone & yrone   iiij[e]

Powder   j last ij Firk'
Salt petir   C di'
Bowes   xxx[ti]
Sheffres of Arowes   lxx[en]
Bowstringes   iij dosein
Morriepickes   xv[en]
Billes   xviij[en]
Crowes of yrone   ij[o]
Pickhammers and Pledgis   iiij[or]
Coiles of Roopes   iiij[or]

Archery weapons and other 'medieval' forms such as bills were still found in the arsenals of these artillery forts, but they may have been stored for use by local militia in times of danger. Indeed, various acts were passed during Henry VIII's reign to ensure that trained archers would be available in the country were it ever to be attacked. Similarly, the presence of pikes and halberds as evidenced from finds at Camber suggest that they, too, were stored for such use.

The documentary record occasionally makes reference to the supply of the castles and fortifications. The *Letters and Papers for May 1545* provide the following example:

Instructions to my lord Suffolk's grace for the blockhouse of Milton, whereof William Burston is captain; being six items of requisites, viz. gunpowder, money for the Performance of the platt [plan], a skilful surveyor of works by advice of Mr. Lee, a commission to take up workmen, ordnance and bows; with request to the Duke in any wise, to remember the powder and two gunners.

Heavy guns as depicted in a late 16th-century manuscript on military science. The Henrician castles were in essence platforms for heavy artillery, offering multiple levels of firepower. (ASKB)

A similar example is provided by the following entry:

List of necessaries for the fortress of Gravesend whereof James Crane, captain, viz. a payer of tinekelles for the bombard, baskets, hurdles, bows, morrispikes, strings, and 12 shot of stone for the bombard of ix inches high, this we have great need of.

In the following month, a warrant was given to the master of the ordnance to deliver 'one last of serpentyne powder' to Philip Bonde, master gunner of Sandsfoot Castle for that castle and nearby Portland Castle. While on January 24, 1546, John Killegrew 'had letters to Sir Thos. Seymour for one last of serpentine powder for the castles of St. Maures and Pendennys by Falmouth'.

OPPOSITE **A gun crew at Pendennis Castle, Cornwall**
This illustration shows the interior of the gun room at Pendennis Castle, Cornwall during firing of the guns. The crew consists of the captain, the master gunner, and two gunner's mates. This cannon is a modern-style muzzle-loading example made of bronze on a wooden mount. Older, wrought-iron, breech-loading models mounted on wooden slides were also used. The ropes attached to the gun allowed it to be pulled back for loading. The gun-port has a wooden shutter; during firing, the gun room would have been filled with choking, acrid smoke.

A gun crew at Pendennis Castle, Cornwall

The castles in war

The invasion scare of 1538–39

The irony of the Henrician castles is that by the time they were completed, the threat they had been intended to counter had passed over, and they were never tested during the reign of Henry VIII. In fact, as early as 1539 when many of the building operations were just getting started, the likelihood of invasion had largely receded, but the king continued with the programme, viewing it as a worthwhile investment for the long-term defence of his realm. As a consequence, a second wave of construction began around the mid 1540s.

Following his excommunication by the Pope in December 1538, Henry 'perceived the evil mind of the Emperor towards him and all the Princes of the Evangelic sort, at the instigation of the Bishop of Rome'. During February 1539, the King's Council met daily to discuss the looming crisis. They were aware of increasing hostility from a variety of European monarchs who viewed the English as heretics. Rumours of war were rife and it appeared that the French and Imperial ambassadors to Henry's court were about to be recalled. The ambassadors did depart the country but the French informed Thomas Cromwell that a replacement would soon arrive. Nonetheless, before his departure, the French ambassador was informed that 'the King was quite able to defend himself', and was shown Cromwell's own armoury as an example of the kind of advanced preparations then in place. Another rumour spread that Francis and Charles were preparing to issue a proclamation forbidding countries to have any dealings with England. Henry retaliated by issuing a similar embargo on March 1 against foreign shipping.

Throughout the realm there was a resolve to defend against this perceived national danger and the country was placed on a war footing. The fortifications of Calais were repaired, and Portsmouth was visited on March 17 where an inventory of bows, arrows and saltpetre was taken in the castle. Musters of local militia were held and beacons prepared on hilltops along the coast. In April, the south coast was surveyed for suitable fortifications, and defensive preparations commenced on the Isle of Wight. As two of the commissioners reported in a letter to Cromwell on March 20, 1539:

> the people of the Isle of Wight … make themselves daily more ready, saying they will stake their coasts and cast their ditches a[new] towards the low water mark that when enemies land it shall be dangerous to them. They will also make bulwarks stronger, and keep their beacons they have set up already on every hill right well.

Early in April 1539 a fleet of ships left the Dutch coast despite a request from the emperor not to depart. False reports came in that the enemy had landed on the Isle of Thanet on the north coast of Kent, but it was enough to convince the English authorities of the need to have enough troops to defend the new forts at Tilbury and Gravesend. As it turned out, the fleet had no designs on England and was merely heading for Spain to take part in the emperor's voyage to Constantinople.

How real was this threat? In the eyes of the English, an invasion was seen as imminent, hence the urgency behind the fortification scheme. Throughout April, ports like Dover were witness to masses of workers constructing new defences, and a visitor to the coast around Deal and Folkestone in May would have seen the extensive preparations then in progress to resist the feared attack. A grand muster was held in London on May 8. As things turned out, the threat receded as quickly as it came, and a case can be made that the king and his chief advisor, Thomas Cromwell, used the perceived threat to distract the country from the current religious crisis which had manifested itself recently in the Pilgrimage of Grace rebellion. Relations with France quickly improved following the arrival of the new ambassador, but the king continued to declare that the threat from the emperor's forces in Flanders was still very real, even though he was probably aware that an invasion would not occur as Charles had many other more pressing needs elsewhere in his dominions.

The French War of 1545

The guns of the new fortifications had remained silent during the first invasion scare, and a gradual malaise fell over the garrisons, but within a few short years the French began again to test the preparedness of England. In 1544, Henry had embarked on a military campaign against Boulogne. The year before, he had sent 12,000 men in support of the emperor against the French in Picardy, and as Charles moved on Paris, Henry successfully besieged Boulogne. It was during this campaign that the king was able to see for himself some of the new features of fortification then taking hold on the Continent. Shortly thereafter, Francis and Charles signed a unilateral peace, leaving the French ready to retaliate against Henry for Boulogne. Once again, fears of an invasion became widespread, and the defeat of an English army by the Scots at Ancrum Moor on the borders near Jedburgh on February 27, 1545 only made matters worse. Sensing this, the French started to make raids against the south coast testing the defences for weaknesses. There was a distinct possibility of an attack on two fronts, from Scotland and from France.

It appeared that Southsea Castle was going to be put to the test on July 18, 1545, when a French fleet of over 200 ships appeared off the east coast of the Isle of Wight, heading up the Solent towards Portsmouth and a showdown with the English fleet. The king was at Portsmouth having arrived to inspect the fleet, and was observing operations the next day when, to his horror, the great warship, *Mary Rose*, was attacked by four enemy galleys. It capsized and sank with her ship's complement of 500 men along with the Vice-Admiral, Sir George Carew.

Henry VIII (centre right) arrives at Southsea Castle on July 19, 1545. (ASKB)

A Henrician castle at war. This detail of Southsea Castle from the Cowdray House engraving is the only contemporary image of a garrison of one of Henry's castles in action as the French are attacking up the Solent in July 1545. (ASKB)

On July 21, the French fleet was observed off Brighton. Soldiers rushed towards the coast in anticipation of a landing and, in fact, the French did land a small force near Newhaven on the 22nd. It is unknown whether Camber Castle saw any action during this action, although the town of Rye had to reimburse the captain of the castle for the loss of three bows 'at the tyme of the contrey commyng in for the defence of our enymes'. In the following year, the government received a request for more gunpowder, which might indicate that supplies had been used up during an engagement in 1545.

In a letter to the Privy Council on July 23, the Captain of the Isle of Wight, Richard Worsley, warned that the enemy will 'attempt Sandoun castle with a camisado [night attack], and land horses there'. The French did in fact put about 2,000 men ashore at four places on the Isle of Wight, including Sandown, the site of one of the new castles then under construction, for Sir Edward Bellyngham made reference to 'labourers' at the place. A few buildings were burnt and shortly after the French sought refuge in a small earthen fortification, possibly St Helen's Fort, built around this time. Fearing being cut off by the English fleet, they began to evacuate. Worsley called out the militia and was able to force the French back to their boats, killing one of their commanders in the process. At Hurst Castle some of the garrison claimed to have heard firing off-shore at the end of July, but by August the threat had passed and the French turned their attention to Boulogne, although there was a naval battle around the 15th of the month off Beachy Head.

During this crisis, emergency plans had been hastily put into operation. Earthworks were quickly erected to defend Portsmouth, and beacons were constructed at likely landing places, 'with the hundreds and men to repair to the same', and 'to appoint a special man to have charge of a number coming to the beacons'. A document from this period includes reference to the preparations at Henry's castles:

For land matters: – In primis, to send for all captains of the blockhouses, and to write that they bring up a note of the state and furniture of their

The French attack the Isle of Wight. The village of Bembridge is burning, while French troops take refuge in a small circular earthen fort at St Helen's, possibly the fortification that was constructed sometime between 1539 and 1552. (ASKB)

houses. Item, for their better manning, and victualling for a fortnight. Item, to know their opinions for men of reputation, and such as shall be agreeable to them, to assist them in case of necessity. Item, to give those men, when they shall be appointed, their charge. Item, to speak with my lord Warden for Rye and Winchelsey and the other places where the Frenchmen landed. Item, to touch the alteration of the state of the soldiers and gunners of the blockhouses.

It is probable that the garrisons of the castles were increased during this period. For instance, the garrison of Camber in January 1544 comprised a captain, six gunners and eight soldiers, a total of 15, but between October and December 1546 it had risen to 29.

Concerned about a sudden attack in the future, the king ordered a number of modifications to be made to Southsea Castle including the creation of eight 'flankers', and gun splays at the foot of the curtain wall to cover any incursion into the dry moat. In addition, the new forts with angled bastions were constructed at Sandown and Yarmouth.

The threat from France continued until June 1546 when hostilities were temporarily halted by a peace treaty. While the garrisons manning Henry's castles were placed on high alert during the crisis, they were not called upon to man their guns, with the possible exceptions of Camber and Southsea. Within a few years, decline and neglect had set in, with the soldiers becoming complacent in their peacetime roles. Garrisons fell below strength and some of the buildings were in need of repair. For instance, an inspection of the Dorset castles in 1574 described Sandsfoot as falling into ruin, with walls cracked by frost and in danger of collapsing into the sea. At Portland, 'both the platforms are in like decay and ruin as the other … and the leads of the same castle is also very much in decay never repaired or renewed since the house was first erected being 34 years past'. Several of the castles had been downsized and had weapons removed. Calshot, for instance, which originally had 36 guns and was considered the most heavily armed of the Solent forts, had only ten serviceable weapons by 1559.

The inventory of 1547

In the year of Henry's death and the succession of his son, Edward VI, an inventory of the king's fortifications was made. Begun in September 1547, the commissioners – Sir William Paulet, Sir John Russell, Sir Walter Mildmay and John, Earl of Warwick – were charged with making an inventory of the ordnance and other munitions in all active castles and fortifications built or refortified during the reign of Henry. The captains of each place were commanded to supply inventories of their commands, and the resulting lists provide an insight into the numbers and kinds of weapons available at the various castles (as noted previously). It was a useful exercise and a gauge of the efficiency of the country's defences, but as things turned out, England subsequently experienced several decades of relative peace.

The Spanish War, 1588–98

As early as 1574, when a Spanish fleet had gathered, a brief survey of the castles had revealed that repairs were needed urgently, but no action was taken. Several years later, a similar survey exposed further deterioration in a number of castles, but it was not until the threat arose from Spain in the 1580s that many were brought back to full strength, re-armed and, in some cases, re-fortified. The castle at Portland was overhauled at a cost of £228, while repairs totalling £50 were carried out at Yarmouth in 1587. The launching of the Armada in 1588 was but the beginning of a campaign by the Spanish against England and various incidents occurred in the 1590s that made the need to strengthen the castles more imperative. Another Spanish fleet sailed in 1596 and only bad weather off Land's End prevented a landing. It turned out that the fleet had been intending to land at Pendennis as a staging post to advance through England. A Privy Council report following a visit by Sir Walter Raleigh and the Earl of Essex concluded that Pendennis was unfit to repel any invaders, prompting immediate action, and in February 1598 four hundred men were sent to work on the castle. They were under the command of Sir Nicholas Parker, and were implementing the designs of Paul Ive who recommended the construction of ramparts on the headland surrounding the Henrician castle.

The Spanish Armada off Start Point, Devon. During the Spanish War of 1588–98, a number of the Henrician castles were overhauled and in some cases additional fortifications were added, as at Pendennis. (ASKB)

A year later, over 100 men were still employed there constructing the bastioned enceinte that surrounds the circular tower. The accession of James I in 1603 finally removed the Spanish threat.

The British Civil Wars, 1642–51

It was not until the civil wars some 40 years later that the structures were properly tested for the first and only time in their histories. How they performed in this conflict is instructive as to their original designs and situations. Many of the Henrician castles endured sieges and some like Pendennis were quite successful in withstanding bombardment. In the years prior to the war, many of the castles had become deserted or were in dire need of repair. In 1626 the garrison of Pendennis was said to be two years in arrears with pay, and living on limpets. Some soldiers apparently succumbed to the poor diet. All the castles were garrisoned at the outset of the conflict in 1642 and were besieged at one time or another. Some fared better than others.

St Mawes Castle, 1646

When the Parliamentarians under General Sir Thomas Fairfax approached St Mawes Castle on March 12, 1646, the castle was already doomed to failure, being positioned below a hill and easily overlooked by enemy guns. The place capitulated without bloodshed after a brief parley between the opposing commanders. That was the only action the castle ever saw.

Pendennis Castle, 1646

In contrast, its sister castle of Pendennis proved a more formidable obstacle to Fairfax, due mainly to the later Elizabethan fortified enceinte and new earthwork defences in front of the entrance across the headland. Six days after capturing St Mawes, the Parliamentarian commander summoned Pendennis to surrender. The Royalist commander, Colonel John Arundell, replied, 'I will here bury myself before I deliver up this castle to such as fight against his Majesty'. Unfortunately for Arundell, his men did not share the same enthusiasm. They were described as 'blades of the right stamp', who 'spare not to be daily drunk, and this the governor encourages'. Nonetheless, when faced with the threat, they responded to the task by keeping fires burning through the night, and 'were very prodigal of their powder, making [firing] two hundred great shot in the space of three days'. The castle was besieged on the ground and blockaded from the sea, which prevented much-needed food and ammunition from St Malo, France being landed.

By July, things were becoming dire and Arundell sent Prince Charles a message that they could not hold out for many more days without relief. Finally, on August 17, 1646 they hauled down the flag and were granted full honours of war, marching out with 'flying colours, trumpets sounding, drums beating, matches lighted at both ends, bullets in their mouths, and every soldier twelve charges of powder'. Twenty-four officers and some 900 other survivors departed the castle.

Had the castle been well supplied, it probably could have withstood a siege for some time. Its location atop a headland gave it a distinct advantage, and the Elizabethan bastioned enceinte provided numerous defended gun positions from which to overlook any attackers. Without these later defences, however, it is doubtful whether the original Henrician castle alone could have held out against artillery bombardment.

Portland Castle, 1643–46

Occupied at the beginning of the war by Parliamentarian troops, the castle changed hands in 1643 following a ruse by a group of Royalists disguised as the enemy. A four-month siege in 1644 was finally ended when a Royalist relieving force showed up. Portland harbour was critical to the Parliamentarian-controlled navy so it was vital that the castle be captured. After the Parliamentarians failed to take it in 1645, it surrendered to Vice-Admiral Batten in April 1646. Why the castle was such a difficult nut to crack is not clear, but its low position just above the waterline may have made it difficult to bombard from the sea.

Southsea Castle, 1642

The Solent castles were occupied but did not experience any fighting. Hurst became the temporary prison for Charles I in December 1648. In contrast, nearby Southsea experienced the war first-hand. Because of its proximity to Royalist-controlled Portsmouth, it was considered of strategic importance by Parliament. It mounted 14 guns facing inland, but had a garrison of only 12 Royalists. In September 1642, a small Parliamentarian force of 400 infantry with two troops of cavalry approached the castle. Some of the attacking force advanced from the sea, several injuring themselves in the process as they jumped into the 5m-deep moat in the process. A Parliamentarian trumpeter sounded a parley but the Royalist governor, a Captain Chaloner, who was suffering from a bout of heavy drinking, asked whether he could surrender the following morning. The besiegers would have none of this and 80 men scaled the walls and easily subdued the small garrison. Three days later, Portsmouth surrendered.

The Downs castles, 1648

The second civil war that broke out in 1648 consisted of a number of regional uprisings and an invasion by the Scots, who were now fighting against Parliament and in support of the king. One of these revolts occurred in Kent and directly involved the Henrician castles of Sandown, Walmer and Deal. These castles were vital for the Parliament-controlled navy as their guns provided shelter for ships at anchor in the Downs. However, in 1648 following the replacement of the popular Vice-Admiral Batten by Colonel Rainsborough, the crews went over to the Royalist cause inspired by Batten himself who had made such overtures to the Scots. In the county itself, word of the landing of a person claiming to be the Prince of Wales on May 19 convinced many to throw in their lot with the Royalists. The Parliamentarian administration was replaced and siege operations were opened against the three castles, which had been reinforced by seamen who had gone ashore on the 26th, but they quickly joined the revolt and were supported by Royalist ships offshore.

A view of Walmer Castle, Kent, from the north-east with an ivy-covered exterior circular bastion in the foreground. The central keep and the tower were rebuilt in the early 18th century, and incorporated the living quarters of the Lord Warden of the Cinque Ports. (PW)

Deal Castle, Kent was designed to work in concert with its sister castles and several earthwork fortifications to protect the important Downs anchorage. This is a view of the dry moat between one of the outer bastions and the curtain wall. Note the gun openings or embrasures. (PW)

Parliament quickly dispatched troops under Colonel Rich to quell the uprising. As one writer put it, 'now by the irony of fate the Castles were to come into action for the first time by meeting an attack by Englishmen from the land'. Rich summoned Deal and Walmer to parley, but the garrisons turned him down. Siege operations were opened against Walmer, but the besiegers had to wait for an engineer and a mortar while standing in trenches full of water and in bitterly cold weather. Nonetheless, they constructed batteries but were harassed by men from Deal and Sandown castles, as well as being attacked from the sea by Royalist ships. Granadoes (mortar-fired metal bombs filled with gunpowder) were fired into the castle and the garrison feigned surrender by opening the gates. Rich's men rushed in only to be confronted by volley fire. A relief of the castle was attempted from the sea but this was beaten back, as was another attack made by 100 men from Deal Castle. Bombarded by granadoes, 16 of which were fired on one day alone, Walmer eventually surrendered on July 12 following a three-week siege.

Rich now turned his attention to Deal where a sally from the garrison was beaten back. Deal proved to be a tougher nut to crack, and the distance between it and Sandown meant that they could not be besieged at the same time. An earthwork fort was constructed between the two in order to command the sea and prevent any relief attempts or attacks from ships. One contemporary account complained about the thickness of Deal's walls, and that both castles had garrisons of around 150 men each including musketeers, amply supplied from ships offshore and under the protection of the castles' guns. It concluded that starving the garrisons was out of the question, and that to achieve a successful outcome would require reducing the castles by bombardment. In late July, the Parliamentarians opened fire on Deal and brought down some battlements. A Royalist landing was repulsed, and on August 7 and 8, the earthwork fort was involved in a fierce artillery duel with the guns of Deal and Sandown castles. As the days wore on, supplies began to dwindle in the castles, as suggested by an intercepted letter from one of the garrison at Deal:

The sea-rogues begin to grumble for want of supplies; if we have not something speedily, or can land, and have some to join us, all is lost: if you hold out you will be brave fellows.

A Royalist landing attempted to relieve the castles but was repulsed with heavy loss, and a valiant last-ditch sally by the garrison of Sandown was met by a volley on August 18. In Deal Castle were many sick and wounded, and the bombardment had damaged much of the masonry. Arrows fired in by the besiegers announced that the Scots had been defeated at Preston. Deal surrendered on August 25, and the garrison marched out; Sandown followed in early September.

An assessment of the castles

The siege of the Downs castles in 1648 is instructive as to how the Henrician fortresses might have fared had they been attacked by the French in the late 1530s and early 1540s. The bombardment by granadoes had a devastating effect on the low-lying masonry, while the difficulty of obtaining fresh provisions caused mounting problems. A siege of such small buildings created very difficult living conditions for the garrisons, many of which had increased in number, and the primitive sanitary arrangements must have created filth and stench, producing appalling conditions. The castles were isolated forts and could easily be surrounded by a determined, well-entrenched besieging force that could not be driven off by ships' guns.

Not all of Henry's castles made such good account of themselves as Deal and Sandown did when it came to the siege warfare of the 17th century. They had been designed to cover important anchorages or likely landing places, rather than to defend against attack from the interior. Such was the case with St Mawes, which had been sited below a hilltop, and Portland, which had all its gun-ports designed to face the harbour. The fact that all the castles survived relatively intact is evidence that it required little to force them to surrender.

An overall assessment of the Henrician style of fortification, based not on how they fared in wartime but in comparison with contemporary developments on the Continent, suggests that they were outdated even before they were completed. There is no denying that the castles maximized offensive firepower with their liberal use of gun-ports, but any advantage they gained on offence was negated by their weak defensive capacity. A person knowledgeable in the science of fortification at the time might have been puzzled at some of the design flaws. Curvilinear bastions festooned with numerous apertures were structurally weak, and as they were arranged in tiers, there would have been a progressive diminishing of firepower as an enemy assault came closer. The fact that they were hollow-walled meant that a sustained heavy bombardment would easily weaken the masonry, with nothing to absorb the shock of the attack. Furthermore, the fact that the bastions in the earliest structures were rounded meant that there would be unflanked dead-ground allowing mining operations to go unhindered. In Italy, such problems had been overcome with the adoption of the angular bastion, yet the speedily constructed fortresses of the 1539 scheme looked backwards rather than forwards. This was probably a result of ignorance of the new forms among the designers and architects of Henry's castles. They were familiar with only England and northern France where the cylindrical tower was the accepted norm.

Nevertheless, these purpose-built platforms showcasing the power of artillery and bristling with gun-ports and embrasures resembled nothing ever built before in England. They served as a transitional form between the tall, medieval castles that had dominated Europe for 500 years, and the low, solid, flat angled-bastioned fortifications that appeared in the later second-phase castles (such as Yarmouth), and became the norm in the late 16th century – a universal form that was to last well into the 19th century.

Aftermath

With the Restoration in 1660, the castles, having avoided the slighting that many earlier structures succumbed to following the civil wars, continued their role as watchdogs of the southern coasts of England, a role that was to continue off and on until the 20th century. Following the internal rebellions of the 17th century, the castles began to decline, although occasional threats from the Continent such as the three Dutch Wars of 1652–54, 1667 and 1679 saw the castles placed once again on a war footing. The Restoration had brought a reduction in the number of men under arms and an overall downsizing of the country's defences. At Yarmouth Castle on the Isle of Wight, the 70-strong garrison was dismissed on four days' notice in 1661, and the guns were removed. It was only later that a small garrison was reconstituted and continued as a small establishment into the succeeding century. Calshot continued to be occupied throughout the 18th century and had a maximum of 25 guns at the opening of the century. Two decades later, the number had fallen to 13, and by the end of the century the surviving guns were described as 'very old and defective', mounted atop rotting carriages. The garrisons of many of the fortifications were considered merely caretakers, but structural modifications were made to a number of the castles during this period. Several had fallen into total disrepair and their location adjacent to the sea meant that coastal erosion had taken its toll. Examples included Sandown Castle in Kent, Camber in Sussex, and Sandsfoot Castle in Dorset. The fort at East Cowes on the Isle of Wight might have been abandoned as early as 1546, while the nearby fort at Sandown had succumbed to the sea and had to be rebuilt.

As for the related earthwork forts and embankments, they suffered from neglect. The Thames estuary forts, especially around the strategic Gravesend–Tilbury crossing, were superseded by new fortifications constructed during the Spanish scare in the 1580s. Elsewhere, the earthworks were abandoned. In fact, as early as

BOTTOM LEFT The Pendennis Artillery Volunteers in an engraving published in 1800, with their commander Lieutenant-Colonel Burgess in the foreground. This special militia artillery unit was created by Governor Melvill during the wars of 1794–1815. The castle is visible in the background. (ASKB)

BOTTOM RIGHT A watercolour depicting Sir William Pitt, Colonel Commandant of the Cinque Port Volunteers in 1804. Behind him can be seen Walmer, while to the left an embankment with an embrasure may be the remains of the earthwork defences that connected the Downs castles. (ASKB)

1547, the four bulwarks connected by a covered way that had been constructed in concert with the Downs castles of Deal, Sandown and Walmer were reported as being 'defaced', and their guns removed to Dover pier. However, three of the forts were still visible in the early 18th century when the noted antiquarian, William Stukeley, sketched the two partially eroded bulwarks and ditches that ran between Walmer and Deal, and the one remaining earthwork fort between Deal and Sandown. The trench or covered way also appears on the edge of an engraving of 1804 depicting William Pitt at Walmer Castle.

During the Napoleonic Wars, several of the castles were garrisoned and their armaments increased. The fortification scheme that saw the erection of numerous Martello towers around the coastline of the British Isles embraced some of the Henrician castles as they were situated in such vulnerable areas. At Sandgate, the central tower of the Henrician castle was rebuilt between 1805 and 1806 as a 'glorified' Martello tower. The roofs of the original keep, the bastions and the half moon were demolished, parts of the original gatehouse removed, and some of the bastions reduced to first-floor levels. Pendennis had raised 'cavaliers' built on the Elizabethan bastions along with additional stores and magazines.

With the return of peace at the end of 1815, the small garrisons were used to aid the Preventative Service in policing the coastline against smuggling. In the mid 1840s and again in the 1860s when fears of a war with France were rampant, the castles were once again called into service to defend the coastline along with the new forts that had been built under the Palmerston government. New emplacements were constructed at Pendennis in 1848 to accommodate three

32-pdr guns. Some of this work continued even when the threat of hostilities had subsided. At Hurst Castle, huge 38-ton guns were installed in the 1870s. Elsewhere, new armament was introduced and occasional modifications and additions were made to modernize the fortifications, to house the new weapons and to improve the living conditions of the garrisons.

In the two major conflicts of the 20th century, many of the castles were pressed into service for the last time. Commanding major anchorages and harbours such as Falmouth and the Solent, they provided suitable platforms on which to mount heavy artillery, searchlights and other military hardware. The advantageous locations of Hurst and Calshot were deemed of strategic importance, as was Pendennis, while the proximity of the French coast meant that Deal, which had been given over to the Office of Works in 1904, and Walmer were ideal for observing the movements of the Dover Patrol in the Great War, and the skies between 1939 and 1945. Home Guard units were now in evidence around the Tudor buildings. During World War II, secret underground defences were carved out of the headland beneath Pendennis Castle. Two tunnels ran approximately 50 yards from the castle to the crescent-shaped Half Moon Battery gun emplacement. St Mawes across the estuary played a significant role with its sister castle, especially during the preparations for the Normandy invasion of 1944, when Falmouth was one of the ports of embarkation. Similarly, Portland Castle, positioned on the water's edge of the vital harbour, was commandeered for use by both British and American military personnel during Operation *Overlord* as living quarters and offices. Eleven years later, it opened to the public as an ancient monument.

In the post-war years, some of the castles continued their military role but manned by various Territorial units rather than the regular army, which practised gunnery from the modern emplacements built around some of the sites. It was not until 1960 that Southsea Castle was finally withdrawn from active service.

Today, we have been left a rich legacy comprising a unique group of artillery forts spaced along the coast of southern England. It is ironic that they represent the results of Henry VIII's onslaught on the great medieval monasteries. Had the king not broken with Rome, today we would probably have fine monastic sites, and no early modern artillery forts.

Two massive wings were added to Hurst Castle in the 1860s to accommodate 30 heavy rifled guns. Hostilities between Britain and France around this period seemed a distinct possibility so the fortifications along the south coast were strengthened. (SW)

The 'One Gun Battery' at Pendennis, built in the late 19th century to accommodate a 6in. 'disappearing gun'. This was removed in 1913, but a battery of 12-pounder guns was positioned here during World War II. (PH)

Visiting the castles today

It is important to reiterate that the remaining castles are the only surviving elements of a much larger fortification scheme involving not only masonry structures but also many earthwork forts, embankments, trenches and ditches, none of which exist today. Similarly, some of the castles have not survived due to demolition, coastal erosion, sea level changes, or incorporation into later structures. These include Sandown, East Cowes, St Helen's and Sharpenode on the Isle of Wight, Brownsea in Dorset, Netley and St Andrew's in Hampshire, Sandown, Milton and Higham in Kent, and West Tilbury and East Tilbury on the south coast of Essex. Many of the surviving sites are owned by the state (English Heritage) or local government and are open to the public (for times of opening, check the websites). Extensive excavations have been carried out at Camber, while small-scale work was undertaken at Sandgate.

Cornwall

Pendennis Castle

Location:	Situated on Pendennis Point, one mile south-east of the centre of Falmouth by road.
OS grid reference:	SW824318.
Length of service:	1540–1956.
Description:	Henrician castle and earlier blockhouse surrounded by an Elizabethan bastioned trace, and later 19th- and 20th-century fortifications, gun emplacements, storehouse and barracks. One of the buildings has been converted into a Discovery Centre detailing the history of the site.
Owner:	English Heritage.
Relevant website:	www.english-heritage.org.uk

St Mawes Castle

Location:	On the Roseland peninsula near the village of St Mawes, two miles east of Falmouth; it can be reached by ferry from Falmouth.
OS grid reference:	SW841327.
Length of service:	1540–1956.
Description:	Henrician castle and earlier blockhouse with later fortifications including the Grand Sea Battery of the Napoleonic period, and a gunpowder magazine of the mid 19th century.
Owner:	English Heritage.
Relevant website:	www.english-heritage.org.uk

Dorset

Portland Castle

Location:	Portland, on the water's edge by the port installations.
OS grid reference:	SY684743.
Length of Service:	1539–1954.
Description:	A small Henrician castle with later additions.
Owner:	English Heritage.
Relevant website:	www.english-heritage.org.uk

Sandsfoot Castle

Location:	Just west of Weymouth by Old Castle Road near the A354.
OS grid reference:	SY674739.

Sandsfoot Castle near Weymouth, Dorset, is situated precariously on cliffs above the bay. Much of the structure is ruinous and will eventually erode away. Originally, it was a two-storey rectangular building connected to a five-sided gun platform commanding the sea. (PL)

Length of service:	1540–1644/45.
Description:	The remains of a small Henrician castle, the ruined parts of which have eroded over the cliff and are dangerous. Sections of outer wall remain in a public park. The adjacent earthworks have been landscaped as public gardens. Access is restricted by railings.
Owner:	Weymouth District Council.
Relevant website:	www.weymouth-dorset.co.uk/sandsfoot.html

Brownsea Castle

Location:	On coast of Brownsea Island facing the mouth of Poole harbour.
OS grid reference:	SZ030876.
Length of service:	1545/47 to the early 18th century.
Description:	A small Henrician blockhouse which was converted into a house around 1718. This was completely rebuilt during the 19th century. Nothing remains of the Henrician fort and small excavations in the basement revealed no deposits.
Owner:	Private.
Relevant website:	www.pastscape.org.uk

Hampshire

Hurst Castle

Location:	On a pebble spit south of Keyhaven.
OS grid reference:	SZ318897.
Length of service:	1541–1933.
Description:	Henrician castle surrounded by later fortifications, mainly consisting of two large wing batteries constructed in the 1860s and designed to house 30 heavy guns, and other later emplacements dating also mainly from the 19th century. The castle was built about 1,700 yards across the Solent from Worsley's Tower (c.1520–38) of which nothing remains today.
Owner:	English Heritage.
Relevant website:	www.english-heritage.org.uk

Calshot Castle

Location:	Two miles south-east of Fawley on a spit where Southampton Water meets the Solent.
OS grid reference:	SU488025.
Length of service:	1539–post 1953.
Description:	Small Henrician castle consisting of a central tower, 15.5m in diameter and 10.5m high, surrounded by later additions including batteries and gatehouse dating from the 18th and 19th centuries.
Owner:	English Heritage.
Relevant website:	www.english-heritage.org.uk

Netley Castle

Location: Near Eastleigh on the southern margin of Southampton.
OS grid reference: SU461088.
Length of service: 1542–c.1627.
Description: Netley Castle is located 250m south-west of the ruins of Netley Abbey. Nothing remains to be seen on the outside as the Henrician fort was incorporated into later buildings. An archaeological watching brief was conducted between winter 1999 and spring 2001; as part of this, small-scale excavations were undertaken.
Owner: Private.
Relevant website: www.archaeology.demon.co.uk/3132.htm

St. Andrew's Castle

Location: In the parish of Hamble on the foreshore.
OS grid reference: SU479059.
Length of service: 1543–1642.
Description: Small artillery castle probably with high, square keep and a low semi-circular bulwark with parapets and a platform, all surrounded by a 25ft-wide moat. All that exists today are fragments of masonry and a breakwater on the shoreline, although the site was excavated in 1971–72.
Relevant website: www.pastscape.org.uk

Southsea Castle

Location: Southsea, on the sea front.
OS grid reference: SZ643980.
Length of service: 1544–1956/60.
Description: Henrician castle with later additions, including a military prison of 1814, a lighthouse of the 1820s, and batteries from the mid and late 19th centuries.
Owner: Portsmouth City Council.
Relevant website: www.southseacastle.co.uk

Isle of Wight

Sharpenode Bulwark

Location: Situated on Sconce Point about 800 yards from the site of Worsley's Tower.
OS grid reference: SZ339898.
Length of service: 1547–1859.
Description: A square earthwork with two angle bastions, rebuilt several times. In the 1840s, it became Fort Victoria.
Owner: Fort Victoria County Park.
Relevant website: www.pastscape.org.uk / www.fortvictoria.co.uk

Yarmouth Castle

Location: Yarmouth, by the quay adjacent to the George Hotel.
OS grid reference: SZ353897.
Length of service: 1547–1901; partially commandeered 1914–45.
Description: A late Henrician castle with an angle bastion and later additions. The site stands next to the George Hotel.
Owner: English Heritage.
Relevant website: www.english-heritage.org.uk

West Cowes Castle

Location: West Cowes.
OS grid reference: SZ493657.
Length of service: 1539–?
Description: This small artillery fort was mostly destroyed by later defences and is now incorporated into the clubhouse of the Royal Yacht Squadron.

Owner: Royal Yacht Squadron.
Relevant website: www.pastscape.org.uk

East Cowes Castle

Location: Unknown.
OS grid reference: SZ511656.
Length of service: 1539–46.
Description: An artillery fort that was abandoned around 1546; the structure was ruinous by the 17th century. Nothing remains above ground today.
Relevant website: www.pastscape.org.uk

St. Helen's Bulwark

Location: Near St Helen's Point.
Length of service: After 1539–1552.
Description: Small earthwork fort; no remains.

Sandown Fort

Location: Sandown.
OS grid reference: SZ604453.
Length of service: 1545–1631.
Description: This Henrician fort was destroyed by the sea and a new fort was built near the site. This was demolished in 1864 and nothing remains above ground today.
Relevant website: www.pastscape.org.uk

The site of West Cowes Castle as it appears today. The remains of the castle were incorporated into the clubhouse of the Royal Yacht Squadron and only the low external wall with embrasures is visible. (SW)

Sussex

Camber Castle (also known as Winchelsea Castle)

Location: One mile south of Rye, one mile across fields off the A259. No access for vehicles.
OS grid reference: TQ921185.
Length of service: 1539–1642; used as a training camp 1939–45.
Description: A large Henrician castle built in three phases around an earlier tower of 1512–14. It is in a ruinous state with associated earthworks, but the site was extensively excavated between 1963 and 1983.
Owner: English Heritage; managed by Rye Harbour Nature Reserve and East Sussex County Council.
Relevant websites: www.english-heritage.org.uk
                      www.wildrye.info/reserve/cambercastle

Kent

Sandgate Castle

Location: Sandgate, near Folkestone, on the sea front.
OS grid reference: TR206351.
Length of service: 1539–1881.
Description: The remains of a Henrician castle are masked by later fortifications including an early 19th-century Martello tower (built 1805–08) and additions dating from 1859 which included a new magazine and alterations to the existing gun emplacements. The castle was requisitioned in both world wars and used as a gun emplacement and bomb shelter for nearby Shorncliffe Barracks. It was undermined by the sea in 1928, and subsequent coastal erosion destroyed about a third of the original castle before a seawall was constructed in the early 1950s. As part of a programme of restoration, the site was partially excavated and cleared of debris between 1976 and 1979.

Owner:	Private; occasionally open to the public.
Relevant website:	www.pastscape.org.uk

Walmer Castle

Location:	Walmer.
OS grid reference:	TR377501.
Length of service:	1539 to present.
Description:	Henrician castle with later fortifications dating from the 1870s, a World War II pillbox, and gardens. It is the official residence of the Lord Warden of the Cinque Ports.
Owner:	English Heritage.
Relevant website:	www.english-heritage.org.uk

Deal Castle

Location:	Deal, on seafront.
OS grid reference:	TR377522.
Length of service:	1539–1951.
Description:	This fine Henrician castle was formerly the official residence of the Captain of the Cinque Ports.
Owner:	English Heritage.
Relevant website:	www.english-heritage.org.uk

Sandown Castle

Location:	Sandown.
OS grid reference:	TR375543.
Length of service:	1539–after 1648.
Description:	This large Downs castle, virtually identical to Walmer, with extensive bulwarks, was ruinous by the late 17th century; it was demolished between 1863 and 1882. Today, only part of the circular keep is still standing.
Owner:	Local government.
Relevant website:	www.pastscape.org.uk

Gravesend Blockhouse

Location:	Gravesham.
OS grid reference:	TQ649744.
Length of service:	1539–53; 1580–19th century.
Description:	A small D-shaped artillery blockhouse that was decommissioned in 1553. It was redeveloped during the late 16th century and subsequently converted into a magazine in the 18th century, but demolished in the 19th century. Following partial excavation, the western two-thirds of the semi-circular front wall with its gun-ports has been consolidated and is on display.
Owner:	Gravesham Borough Council.
Relevant website:	www.pastscape.org.uk

Milton Blockhouse

Location:	Gravesham.
OS grid reference:	TQ652743.
Length of service:	1539–1553.
Description:	A blockhouse and artillery castle built in 1539, with a later angle bastion facing inland built c.1545. It was decommissioned in 1553 and demolished between 1557 and 1558. The site was located by archaeological excavations between 1974 and 1978. Nothing is visible above ground today.
Owner:	Gravesham Borough Council.
Relevant website:	www.pastscape.org.uk

Higham Blockhouse

Location:	Unknown but probably on the west bank of Shorne Creek where it connects with the River Thames.
OS grid reference:	Possibly TQ77.

Length of service: 1539–53.
Description: A small artillery blockhouse built between 1539 and 1541 to work in concert with the blockhouse at East Tilbury (Essex). The fort was decommissioned in 1553 and demolished between 1557 and 1558. Nothing remains to be seen above ground.

Essex

West Tilbury Blockhouse
Location: In the parish of Chadwell St Mary.
OS grid reference: TQ650755.
Length of service: 1539–53; 1580–1945.
Description: A small D-shaped artillery blockhouse standing within an irregular moated enclosure that was decommissioned in 1553, was remodelled in 1580–81, and was 'in great decay' by 1558. It was rcompletely rebuilt by Sir Bernard de Gomme beginning in 1670. The Tudor fort, however, remained standing within the later fort until around 1867. Today the site lies buried under the later fort.
Owner: English Heritage.
Relevant website: www.english-heritage.org.uk

East Tilbury Blockhouse
Location: In the parish of East Tilbury.
OS grid reference: TQ691761.
Length of service: 1539–53.
Description: A small artillery blockhouse built between 1539 and 1541 to work in concert with the blockhouse at Higham (Kent). By 1735 the site had been inundated by the sea and is shown just offshore on a contemporary map. It is possible that the remains of the site lie beneath the mud.
Owner: Offshore scheduled site.
Relevant website: www.pastscape.org.uk

Bibliography

Anglo, S. 'The Hampton Court Painting of the Field of Cloth of Gold, *Antiquaries Journal* Vol. XLVI (2), 287–307 (London, 1966).

Biddle, M., Hiller, J., Scott, I., and Streeten, A. *Henry VIII's Coastal Artillery Fort at Camber Castle, Rye, East Sussex: An Archaeological Structural and Historical Investigation* (Oxford Archaeological Unit for English Heritage, London, 2001).

Brewer, J. S. (ed.), *Letters and Papers, Foreign and Domestic of the Reign of Henry VIII* (HMSO, London, 1862–1920).

Brooks, S. *Southsea Castle* (Pitkin, Andover, 1996).

Coad, J. G. *Calshot Castle, Kent* (English Heritage, London, 1996).

Coad, J. G. *Deal Castle, Kent* (English Heritage, London, 2000).

Coad, J. G. *Hurst Castle, Hampshire* (English Heritage, London, 2001).

Colvin, H. M. (ed.) *The History of the King's Works, IV, 1485–1600*, Part II (HMSO, London, 1982).

Dürer, Albrecht *Etliche underricht zu befestigung der Stett, Schlosz, und flecken.* (Nurenberg, 1527). With the addition of an introduction by Martin Biddle (Gregg, Farnborough, 1972).

Fissel, M. *English Warfare, 1511–1642* (Routledge, London, 2001).

Fynmore, R. J. *Sandgate Castle, Kent* (n.d.)

Harris, E. C. 'Archaeological investigations at Sandgate Castle, Kent, 1976–9', *Post-Medieval Archaeology* Vol. 14, 53–88 (London, 1980).

Kenyon, J. R. 'A Note on Two Original Drawings by William Stukeley Depicting "The three Castles which keep the Downs"', *Antiquaries Journal* Vol. 58, 162–64 (London, 1978).

Kenyon, J. R. 'Ordnance and the King's Fortifications in 1547–48', *Archaeologia* Vol. 107, 165–213 (London, 1982).

Lawson, S. (ed.) *Portland Castle, Dorset* (English Heritage, London, 2000).

Lawson, S. (ed.) *Walmer Castle and Gardens* (English Heritage, London, 2003).

Linzey, R. *The Castles of Pendennis and St Mawes* (English Heritage, London, 2004).Longmate, N. *Island Fortress: The defence of Great Britain 1603–1945* (London, Hutchinson, 1991).

Morley, B. M. *Henry VIII and the Development of Coastal Defence* (HMSO, London, 1976).

Netley Castle, Hampshire. Archaeological Watching Brief Winter 1999–Spring 2001 (www.archaeology.demon.co.uk/3132.htm)

O'Neil, B. H. St John, *Castles and Canon: A Study of Early Artillery Fortifications in England* (Oxford, 1960).

O'Neil, B. H. St John 'Stefan von Haschenperg, an Engineer to King Henry VIII, and his work', *Archaeologia* Vol. 91, 137–55 (London, 1945).

Parker, G. *The Military Revolution. Military innovation and the rise of the west, 1500–1800* (CUP, Cambridge 1988).

Powell, J. R. 'The Siege of the Downs Castles in 1648', *The Mariner's Mirror* Vol. 51 (2), 155–71 (London, 1965).

Rigold, S. E. *Yarmouth Castle, Isle of Wight* (English Heritage, London, 2003).

Saunders, A. 'Coastal Defences since the Introduction of Artillery', *Archaeological Journal* Vol. 123, 136–171 (London, 1966).

Saunders, A. *Dartmouth Castle* (Department of the Environment, London, 1965).

Saunders, A. *Fortress Britain: Artillery fortification in the British Isles and Ireland* (Beaufort Publishing Ltd., 1989).

Shelby, J. *John Rogers. Tudor Military Engineer* (OUP, Oxford, 1967).

Smith, V. T. C. 'The Milton Blockhouse, Gravesend: Research and Excavation', *Archaeologia Cantiana* Vol. XCVI, 341–62 (London, 1980).

Thompson, D. and Smith, V. 'The Excavation of the Gravesend Blockhouse, 1975–76', *Archaeologia Cantiana* Vol. XCIII, 153–77 (London, 1977).

Thompson, M. W. *The Decline of the Castle* (CUP, Cambridge, 1987).

Additional articles covering this period are available in the journals *Fort* and *Port-Medieval Archaeology*. Information about individual sites (sources, visitor information, location, investigation history, aerial photographs, maps, etc.) is available from English Heritage's Pastscape website, the online database for the National Monuments Record (www.pastscape.org.uk).

Glossary

ashlar Large, squared blocks of dressed stone laid in regular courses.

bastion Defensive structure projecting from a fortification whether semi-circular in the earlier works or angular later.

battery Earth or masonry platform for mounting guns or mortars.

blockhouse A small timber or masonry detached fortification.

bulwark A small fortification generally built out of earth and wood. Can also refer to bastions.

buttress Masonry projection from a wall to provide additional strength.

casemate Vaulted room under a rampart for protecting guns and for garrison accommodation.

castle Medieval term still used in 16th century for a large masonry fortification.

caponier Covered communication passage in the moat of a fort often with loopholes.

cavalier A work raised higher than the ramparts to command the surrounding countryside.

counterscarp The outer side of a defensive ditch, i.e. facing the defenders.

covered way A protected ditch or passageway allowing communication.

curtain Outer wall of a fortification or castle.

enceinte The body of an area or place enclosed within its ramparts and parapets, but excluding its outworks.

embrasure Opening in a wall or earthen bank to allow a cannon to be fired.

enfilading fire Fire which sweeps the whole length of a fortification.

flank A length of work facing towards adjacent defence from which to provide covering fire.

flanker A gun mounted in a flank or side of bastion designed to fire along the front of the connecting curtain wall.

gabions Baskets filled with earth as a protection for cannon.

garderobe A latrine, often located in an exterior wall.

glacis A slope outside a defence on which attackers are exposed to fire.

gorge The rear part of any fortification, whether open or closed; often the neck of a bastion.

gun-port A small opening in a wall to allow hand-held weapons to be fired through.

half-moon An outwork, usually rounded.

keep A main central tower, often circular or square, and the last place to defend in time of siege.

loop A small opening for shooting firearms.

magazine An ammunition store.

palisade Sharpened wooden stakes often surmounting an earthwork.

parapet A low wall on top of a curtain wall, bastion, or keep, designed to provide shelter for gunners or soldiers.

plat (plott) A map or chart laying out castle plans.

platform A solid surface of masonry or timber to provide a firm footing for artillery.

portcullis A vertical grill made of iron or wood that can be lowered down in grooves to block the entrance to a castle or fortification.

postern A secondary gateway.

rampart A bank of earth or masonry, often derived from the excavation of an outer ditch surrounding a fortification and providing protection for the garrison.

saker A type of cannon.

salient angle The angle of a bastion pointing towards the field.

sally-port A subsidiary gate, often concealed, through which the garrison can 'sally out' to attack the besieging force.

scarp The inner side of a defensive ditch, i.e. the one facing the attacking force.

splay The sides of a window, door or gun-port where the opening widens towards the inner or outer face of the wall.

wall-walk A walkway on the top of a wall protected by a parapet or battlements.

work A term used in military manuals for any form of defence.

Index

References to illustrations are shown in **bold**.